First World War
and Army of Occupation
War Diary
France, Belgium and Germany

74 (YEOMANRY) DIVISION
230 Infantry Brigade
Headquarters
1 May 1918 - 29 May 1919

WO95/3153/1

The Naval & Military Press Ltd
www.nmarchive.com
Published in association with The National Archives

Published by

The Naval & Military Press Ltd

Unit 10 Ridgewood Industrial Park,
Uckfield, East Sussex,
TN22 5QE England
Tel: +44 (0) 1825 749494

www.naval-military-press.com
www.nmarchive.com

This diary has been reprinted in facsimile from the original. Any imperfections are inevitably reproduced and the quality may fall short of modern type and cartographic standards.

Contents

Document type	Place/Title	Date From	Date To
Heading	WO95/3153/1 Headquarters		
Heading	74th Division 230th Infy Bde Bde Headquarters 1918 May-May 1919		
Heading	Headquarters 230th Inf. Bde (74th Division) May 1918		
Heading	British Salonika Force War Diary		
War Diary	On Board S.S. Malwa at Alexandria	01/05/1918	10/05/1918
War Diary	Ponthoile	11/05/1918	27/05/1918
War Diary	Izel Les Hameau	28/05/1918	31/05/1918
Operation(al) Order(s)	230th Infantry Brigade Administrative Order No. 11	19/05/1918	19/05/1918
Operation(al) Order(s)	230th Infantry Brigade Order No. 42	24/05/1918	24/05/1918
Miscellaneous	Medical Arrangements	21/05/1918	21/05/1918
Miscellaneous	Messages And Signals		
Miscellaneous	Reference Attached Entraining Details		
Miscellaneous	Move Of 74th (Yeomanry) Division, May 20th. 1918		
Heading	Headquarters 230th Inf. Bde. (74th Division) June 1918		
Heading	British Salonika Force War Diary 26th Division		
War Diary	Izel-Les-Hameaux	01/06/1918	27/06/1918
War Diary	Flechin	27/06/1918	30/06/1918
Heading	Headquarters 230th Inf. Bde (74th Division) July 1918		
Heading	British Salonika Force War Diary 27th Division		
War Diary	Flechin	01/07/1918	14/07/1918
War Diary	Chateau Beaulieu	15/07/1918	23/07/1918
War Diary	Ham. En Artois	24/07/1918	31/07/1918
Operation(al) Order(s)	230th Infantry Brigade Order No. 41	10/07/1918	10/07/1918
Miscellaneous	Relief Table Issued With 230th Infantry Brigade Order No. 41.	10/07/1918	10/07/1918
Operation(al) Order(s)	230th Infantry Brigade Order No. 43	10/07/1918	10/07/1918
Operation(al) Order(s)	230th Infantry Brigade Order No. 44	17/07/1918	17/07/1918
Miscellaneous	Messages And Signals.		
Operation(al) Order(s)	230th Infantry Brigade Order No. 46	20/07/1918	20/07/1918
Operation(al) Order(s)	230th Infantry Brigade Order No. 45	20/07/1918	20/07/1918
Miscellaneous	Relief Table Issued With 230th Infantry Brigade Order No. 45.	20/07/1918	20/07/1918
Operation(al) Order(s)	230th Inf. Bde. Order No. 45.	20/07/1918	20/07/1918
Operation(al) Order(s)	Relative To 230th Infantry Brigade Order No. 45	20/07/1918	20/07/1918
Miscellaneous	List Of Papers Handed Over To 229th Inf. Bde	24/07/1918	24/07/1918
Miscellaneous	Relief Table Issued With 230th Infantry Brigade Order No. 45	20/07/1918	20/07/1918
Operation(al) Order(s)	230th Infantry Brigade Order No. 45	20/07/1918	20/07/1918
Operation(al) Order(s)	230th Infantry Brigade Order No. 46	20/07/1918	20/07/1918
Heading	Headquarters 230th Inf. Bde (74th Division) August 1918		
Miscellaneous	British Salonika Force War Diary		
Miscellaneous	Headquarters 74th (Yeo) Division		
War Diary	Hamen Artois	01/08/1918	05/08/1918
War Diary	P.T.C.	05/08/1918	09/08/1918
War Diary	Lahaye	09/08/1918	09/08/1918
War Diary	P.II.a	09/08/1918	09/08/1918
War Diary	Lahaye Fm	10/08/1918	17/08/1918
War Diary	Busne Chateau	17/08/1918	21/08/1918

War Diary	Lahaye	22/08/1918	25/08/1918
War Diary	P.T.C	26/08/1918	26/08/1918
War Diary	St H.Laire	26/08/1918	29/08/1918
War Diary	Baisieux	30/08/1918	31/08/1918
War Diary	Map 620 1.40000 A 23. Camp		
Operation(al) Order(s)	230th Infantry Brigade Order No. 47.	01/08/1918	01/08/1918
Miscellaneous	Relief Table	01/08/1918	01/08/1918
Operation(al) Order(s)	230th Infantry Brigade Order No. 47	01/08/1918	01/08/1918
Operation(al) Order(s)	230th Infantry Brigade Order No. 48	06/08/1918	06/08/1918
Operation(al) Order(s)	230th Infantry Brigade Order No. 50	10/08/1918	10/08/1918
Operation(al) Order(s)	230th Infantry Brigade Order No. 51	11/08/1918	11/08/1918
Operation(al) Order(s)	230th Brigade Order No. 52	12/08/1918	12/08/1918
Miscellaneous	Messages And Signals		
Miscellaneous	B.m. 230th Inf. Bde		
Operation(al) Order(s)	230th Infantry Brigade Order No. 53	13/08/1918	13/08/1918
Operation(al) Order(s)	230th Infantry Brigade Order No. 54	15/08/1918	15/08/1918
Miscellaneous	Relief Table		
Operation(al) Order(s)	230th Infantry Brigade Order No. 54	15/08/1918	15/08/1918
Miscellaneous	230th Infantry Brigade Battle Instructions No.2	16/08/1918	16/08/1918
Miscellaneous	230th Infantry Brigade Order No. I	15/08/1918	15/08/1918
Operation(al) Order(s)	230th Infantry Brigade Order No. 55	21/08/1918	21/08/1918
Operation(al) Order(s)	230th Infantry Brigade Order No. 56	21/08/1918	21/08/1918
Operation(al) Order(s)	230th Infantry Brigade Order No. 57	23/08/1918	23/08/1918
Miscellaneous	Movement Table		
Operation(al) Order(s)	230th Infantry Brigade Order No. 58	25/08/1918	25/08/1918
Miscellaneous	March Table		
Operation(al) Order(s)	230th Infantry Brigade Order No. 58	25/08/1918	25/08/1918
Miscellaneous	230th Infantry Brigade Group		
Heading	Headquarters 230th Inf. Bde. (74th Division) September 1918		
Miscellaneous	British Salonika Force.War Diary		
War Diary	1. A 23 Cent	01/09/1918	01/09/1918
War Diary	C 25 B 42	02/09/1918	05/09/1918
War Diary	J1a 4.5.	05/09/1918	07/09/1918
War Diary	Templeux La Fosse	07/09/1918	12/09/1918
War Diary	D30b 77	12/09/1918	18/09/1918
War Diary	The Quarries	19/09/1918	20/09/1918
War Diary	Templeux Quarries	21/09/1918	26/09/1918
War Diary	Fouilloy	27/09/1918	28/09/1918
War Diary	Allouagne	28/09/1918	30/09/1918
Miscellaneous	With Reference To Brigade Order No. 67	16/09/1918	16/09/1918
Operation(al) Order(s)	230th Infantry Brigade Order No. 67	16/09/1918	16/09/1918
Miscellaneous	230th Infantry Brigade Battle Instructions No.3	16/09/1918	16/09/1918
Miscellaneous	230th Infantry Brigade Battle Instructions No.2	16/08/1918	16/08/1918
Miscellaneous	230th Infantry Brigade Battle Instructions No.1	15/08/1918	15/08/1918
Miscellaneous	230th Infantry Brigade Battle Instructions No.4	17/09/1918	17/09/1918
Operation(al) Order(s)	230th Infantry Brigade Order No. 69	20/09/1918	20/09/1918
Miscellaneous	Addenda No, 3. To Brigade Order No, 71.	29/09/1918	29/09/1918
Heading	Headquarters, 230th Inf. Bde. (74th Division) October 1918		
Miscellaneous	British Salonika Force War Diary		
War Diary	Allouagne	01/10/1918	03/10/1918
War Diary	S10 X	03/10/1918	04/10/1918
War Diary	Herlies	04/10/1918	31/10/1918
Operation(al) Order(s)	Brigade Order No. 72	02/10/1918	02/10/1918
Operation(al) Order(s)	230th Infantry Brigade Order No. 73	06/10/1918	06/10/1918

Operation(al) Order(s)	230th Infantry Brigade Order No. 74	08/10/1918	08/10/1918
Miscellaneous	Addenda No.1. To Brigade Order No. 74.	09/10/1918	09/10/1918
Miscellaneous	Addenda No.2. Brigade Order No. 74.	09/10/1918	09/10/1918
Operation(al) Order(s)	230th Infantry Brigade Order No. 76.	12/10/1918	12/10/1918
Operation(al) Order(s)	230th Infantry Brigade Order No. 78.	20/10/1918	20/10/1918
Operation(al) Order(s)	230th Infantry Brigade Order No. 79.	24/10/1918	24/10/1918
Operation(al) Order(s)	230th Infantry Brigade Order No. 80	25/10/1918	25/10/1918
Operation(al) Order(s)	230th Infantry Brigade Operation Order No. 81.	27/10/1918	27/10/1918
Operation(al) Order(s)	230th Infantry Brigade Operation Order No. 82	29/10/1918	29/10/1918
Operation(al) Order(s)	230th Infantry Brigade Operation Order No. 82.	27/10/1918	27/10/1918
Operation(al) Order(s)	230th Inf. Brigade Order No. 83.	29/10/1918	29/10/1918
Miscellaneous	230th Infantry Brigade Special Instructions	03/11/1918	03/11/1918
Miscellaneous	230th Infantry Brigade Special Instructions	30/10/1918	30/10/1918
Operation(al) Order(s)	230th Infantry Brigade Order No. 84	06/11/1918	06/11/1918
Operation(al) Order(s)	230th Infantry Brigade Order No. 84	31/10/1918	31/10/1918
Miscellaneous	Defence Scheme	28/10/1918	28/10/1918
Miscellaneous	230th Infantry Brigade Special Instructions	03/11/1918	03/11/1918
Miscellaneous	230th Infantry Brigade Special Instructions	30/10/1918	30/10/1918
Heading	Headquarters 230th Inf. Bde (74th Division) November 1918		
Miscellaneous	Cover For Branch Memoranda.		
Miscellaneous	Headquarters 74th Division		
War Diary		01/11/1918	20/11/1918
Heading	Headquarters 230th Inf Bde (74th Division) December 1918		
Miscellaneous	British Salonika Force War Diary		
Miscellaneous	Headquarters 74th (Yeomanry) Division	06/01/1919	06/01/1919
War Diary		01/12/1918	26/01/1919
War Diary	Gammerages	28/01/1919	31/03/1919
War Diary	Grammont	04/04/1919	29/05/1919

WO 95/3153/1

Headquarters'

74TH DIVISION
230TH INFY BDE

BDE HEADQUARTERS

1918 MAY - ~~DEC 1918~~
~~JAN~~ - MAY 1919

Vol. 2

Headquarters,
230th Inf. Bde
(74th Division)

May 1918.

169 Inf Bde

Sept 1917.

Volume No. ....

BRITISH SALONIKA FORCE

WAR DIARY.

27th Division

Vol. No.	Unit	PERIOD From	To
14.	80th Trench M. Battery.	1.4.18	30.4.18
18.	81st do.	"	"
19.	82nd do.	"	"

A.P. & S.D., Alex./No. 752/8:5:17/3000 (50041G/53) W. M. & Co.

1. 230 Inf Bde

BEF

WAR DIARY
or
INTELLIGENCE SUMMARY.
(*Erase heading not required.*)

Army Form C. 2118.

May 1918 HQ 230 Infy Bde

Vol 2

Instructions regarding War Diaries and Intelligence Summaries are contained in F. S. Regs., Part II. and the Staff Manual respectively. Title pages will be prepared in manuscript.

Place	Date	Hour	Summary of Events and Information	Remarks and references to Appendices
On board SS. MALWA at ALEXANDRIA	1		GOC and Div. Staff came on board MALWA.	
			No officers or OR allowed ashore.	
		1015	Boat drill and life belt inspection.	
		1430	Convoy sailed consisting of SS. CANBERRA, CALEDONIA, MALWA, KAISER-I-HIND, LEASOWE CASTLE & OMRAH escorted by destroyers H.J.M. [illegible]	
			Monitor with Observation balloon accompanied us till dusk & then returned.	
	2		Men fairly comfortable but crowded, food for all [illegible] good	
	3 4.	1800	Passed convoy 17 ships travelling in opposite direction. Two extra destroyers joined us.	
	7		Convoy arrived MARSEILLES, after no excitements. Bde landed and marched to No 10 Rest Camp MONTFERAN.	
			Staff Capt left with Div HQrs for NOYELLES.	
	8		BGC. BMa B.I.O. left by "rapide" for [struck through] NOYELLES	
	9		Bde left Rest Camp for NOYELLES by train	
	10	0500	BGC. BM. Div HQ & S.C. arrived NOYELLES.	
			BGC BM & S.C. went round billets and saw the transport officers who had arrived about a week before with transport by another convoy. Billets all occupied.	

[illegible] Brigadier General 230 Inf Bde

D. D. & L., London, E.C. (A8004) Wt. W1771/M2 31 750,000 5/17 Sch. 52 Forms/C2118/14

230 INF BDE

B.E.F.

WAR DIARY
or
~~INTELLIGENCE SUMMARY.~~
(Erase heading not required.)

MAY 1918

Army Form C. 2118.

Instructions regarding War Diaries and Intelligence Summaries are contained in F. S. Regs., Part II. and the Staff Manual respectively. Title pages will be prepared in manuscript.

Place	Date	Hour	Summary of Events and Information	Remarks and references to Appendices
~~NOUVIONS~~ PONTHOILE	11	0800	BHQ & 7th MG Bn arrived NOYELLES billetted at PONTHOILE & Stage Camp NOUVIONS respectively.	
		1100	10 Buffs arrived and billetted at FOREST L'ABBAYE	
	12.	0720	12 Norfolks and 7/15 Suffolks arrived & went into rest camp	
		0830	NOYELLES till 0830 when they proceeded to billets, Norfolks to Staging Camp NOUVIONS, Suffolks to LAMOTTE BULEUX.	
		1700	GOC called — 7/Suffolks 16 Sussex arrived, Sussex billetted at MORLAY	
		1930	Div Gas Officer called and arranged for gas lectures & drill.	
	13.	1000	BGC, BM & SC called on Buffs in billets.	
		1330.	BGC met C in C at Div HQrs went in car with BGC HOARE.	
	14.	0900	All day gas instruction by VII Corps Chemical advisor to 16 Sussex at MORLAY, attended by BHQ. LTMB.	
	14	1600	Lecture by Lt Col CAMPBELL to Buffs and ~~Norfolks~~ Suffolks at NOUVIONS on bayonet fighting	
	15		Gas instruction to Suffolks at LAMOTTE-BULEUX.	
		1200	Lecture by Lt Col Campbell at MORLAY - to Sussex and Norfolks	
	16.		Gas instruction to Norfolks at NOUVIONS	
	17		Lt Col A.F. MORSE arrived and assumed command of 12 Norfolks.	
			Gas Instruction to Norfolks.	
		2100	Gas projector demonstration to Buffs Norfolks Suffolks MG Bn officers at NOUVIONS	
	18		Gas instruction to Buffs at FOREST L'ABBAYE	

[illegible] Major
Brigade Major 230 Inf Bde

D. D. & L., London, E.C. (A8004) Wt. W1771/M2 31 750,000 5/17 Sch 52 Forms/C2118/14

3.

230 INF BDE

Instructions regarding War Diaries and Intelligence Summaries are contained in F. S. Regs., Part II. and the Staff Manual respectively. Title pages will be prepared in manuscript.

B.E.F.

WAR DIARY
or
~~INTELLIGENCE SUMMARY.~~
~~(Erase heading not required.)~~

MAY.
1918

Army Form C. 2118.

Place	Date	Hour	Summary of Events and Information	Remarks and references to Appendices
POINTHOILE ~~BUNEVILLE~~	MAY 19	0800	Staff Capt and representatives went on to new area S of St POL in a lorry –	
			G.O.C. called in the evening.	
	20	noon	MAJOR WEAKES from G.H.Q. called.	
		1500	GSO1 & GSO2 called –	
			Entraining orders received.	
	21.	2134	B.H.Q. entrained with 1 Coy each of Buffs, Norfolks, & Suffolks	
			3 Detraining officers accompanied BHQ & undertook detraining of Bde at LIGNY under Lt. HOPWOOD. & Capt J. HARBORD 12 Norfolks.	
			3 Officers under Capt K HOLLEBONE 10 Buffs supervised Bde Training at RUE.	
	22.		During the day, the whole of the Group arrived in new area & were billetted as follows B.H.Q. BUNEVILLE – 10 Buffs BUNEVILLE – 12 Norfolks MAISNIL-St POL – NEUVILLE AU CORNET 15 Suffolks MAISNIL-St POL & HERLIN-LE-SEC 16 Sussex FOUFFLIN-RICAMETZ – LTMB MONTS EN TERNOIS – RMRE Pt HOUVIN – 449 Co ASC FOUFFIN-RICAMETZ – 230 F.Amb MONTS EN TERNOIS. Div H.Q. ROELLECOURT.	
	23.		BGC inspected "D" Coy of 15th Suffolks at MAISNIL.	
		1600	Conference of Cos and 2nds in Command.	
	24.		Rained.	
			Received orders for Bde Group to proceed to IZEL-LES-HAMEAU tomorrow.	
			S.C. with representatives went on ahead to arrange billets.	
	25.		Bde marched independently as per orders attached "A"	APP. A. March orders attached)
			Complete in new area by 1.30 pm. Billetted as follows:–	
			B.H.Q 10 Buffs & 12 Norfolks at IZEL-LES-HAMEAU – 15 Suffolks PENIN – 16 Sussex at MANIN. 230 LTMB, F.Amb & RMRE at VILLERS-SIR-SIMON – 449 Co ASC at DOFFINE – MGC marched to BEAUFORT and joined 229 Bde Group.	
	27		Training in neighbourhood of billets – BGC Bde visited training areas and looked at ranges. One range allotted to each Bn daily	

[illegible] Major
Bde Maj
30 Jun 18

4

Instructions regarding War Diaries and Intelligence Summaries are contained in F. S. Regs., Part II. and the Staff Manual respectively. Title pages will be prepared in manuscript.

230 INF. BDE

BEF

WAR DIARY

or

~~INTELLIGENCE SUMMARY.~~

~~(Erase heading not required.)~~

MAY 1918

Army Form C. 2118.

Place	Date	Hour	Summary of Events and Information	Remarks and references to Appendices
IZEL LES HAMEAU	May 28.		GOC 74 Div inspected all Bns in vicinity of billets at following times 9 am 16 Sussex. 1030 10 Buffs & 12 R Norfolks. 230. 15 Suffolks. 10 Buffs well turned out. 12 Norfolks clothing bad.	
	29	1700	Bde attended BGs conference at Div HQrs.	
	30.	1700	Conference of COs & 2nds in C at BHQ.	
	31.	1000	BGC inspected 1 Coy of 16 Sussex.	
		1700	BGC " " 10 Buffs.	
			Capt R.A. LESLIE left BHQ to undertake duties of Div Bath's officer.	
			Lt Col LORD SACKVILLE left to be attached to [illegible] G.H.Q.	
			Party of officers left for attachment to NEW ZEALAND Div for experience in the line. Following went: O.C. 10 Buffs & 16 Sussex with 4 Coy Cmdrs each & 2 G officers and 2 officers from LTMB.	
			Effective Strengths at date: 10 Buffs 40 Off 854 OR; 12 Norfolks 37 " 796 "; 15 Suffolks 37 " 904 "; 16 Sussex 41 " 857 "	
			The health of the troops has been good during the month, in all 6 officers & 290 OR have been evacuated sick.	
			[illegible] Major Bde Major 230 Inf Bde	

(A7092). Wt. W12839/M1293. 750,000. 1/17. D. D. & L., Ltd. Forms/C.2118/14.

SECRET.

230th INFANTRY BRIGADE ADMINISTRATIVE ORDER No.11.
to be read in conjunction with

74th DIVISION ADMINISTRATIVE INSTRUCTIONS, C.A/174 of 19/5/18.

Para 3. Entraining and detraining Officers will be detailed by Battalions as below:-

ENTRAINING OFFICERS.

10th Buffs. 1 Capt. and 1 Subaltern.
16th Sussex 1 Subaltern.

These Officers will arrive at RUE Station by 6.p.m on 21st inst and will supervise the entraining of the Bde.Group under the direction of the Capt.detailed by the Buffs. One of these Officers at least will be on duty at a time.

DETRAINING OFFICERS.

12th Norfolks. 1 Capt. and 1 Subaltern.
15th Suffolks. 1 Subaltern.

These Officers will travel by the 21.34 train with Bde.H.Q. on the 21st inst and will supervise the detraining of the Bde.Group.
C.O. detraining party will report complete arrival of the Bde. Group to Bde.H.Q.
Names of entraining and detraining Officers detailed will be notified to Bde,H.Q. by 11.a.m. tomorrow,21st inst.

Para.6. Each Infantry Battalion will be supplied with 2 Baggage and 2 Supply wagons - the M.G.Bn. with one of each.
These wagons will report to Units at 5.p.m. today,20th.
One N.C.O. and one Artificer will be attached to each Unit for the journey and should be included in the entraining state.

Para.7. Motor Lorries will be at the disposal of Units as under at the times stated. These lorries should be loaded and proceed to RUE and then unloaded as quickly as possible as they have to make several journeys.

1 Lorry will report to the Suffolks at 3.30.p.m. 21st.
1 " " " " " Buffs " " " "
1 " " " " " Norfolks " " " "

These will be used by the party proceeding by train No.10.
also
2 Lorries will report to Suffolks at 7.p.m. 21st
2 " " " " Norfolks at 11.p.m. 21st.
1 " " " " L.T.M.B. at 12.midnight.
2 " " " " Buffs at 3.a.m. 22nd.
2 " " " " Sussex at 7.a.m. 22nd.
1 " " " " 74th M.G.Bn. at 7.a.m.22nd.
1 " " " " R.M.R.E. at 7.a.m.22nd.

GUIDES. The Suffolks will send 2 guides to report at present Bde.H.Q. at 3.p.m.21st, the Norfolks will send one at 3.p.m. and another to report at 10.p.m.,The Buffs one at 3.p.m. and one at or before midnight 21st/22nd. The Sussex will send 3 guides at 6.a.m. on the 22nd and L.T.M.B will send 1 guide at or before midnight 21st/22nd.
74th M.G.Bn. and the R.M.R.E. will send guides to report to Bde.H.Q. at 6.a.m. 22nd.

ACKNOWLEDGE

Major,
Brigade Major.
230th Infantry Brigade.

20th May 1918.

Copies cont'd. No.6. 16th Sussex.
7. L.T.M.Battery
8. M.G.Battalion.
9. 230th Fd.Ambce.
10. R.M.R.E.
11. 449th Coy.A.S.C.
12. 230th Bde.H.Q.
13. War Diary.
14. do
15. do
16. "Q"

APPA

SECRET. Copy No. 16

230TH INFANTRY BRIGADE ORDER No.42.

Reference:- LENS, Sheet 11. 1.100,000.

24th May 1918.

1. 230th Infantry Brigade will move to PENIN - GIVENCHY-le-NOBLE - IZEL-les-HAMEAU tomorrow, 25th inst.
   The M.G.Battalion will march to BEAUFORT and will be transferred to the 229th Bde.Group.

2. Units will not move East of the line GRAND BULLECOURT - AMBRINES - AVERDOINGT before 10 a.m.

3. Distances on the march will be maintained as under:-

Between Battalions	500 yards.	
" Companies	100	"
" Unit and its transport	100	"

4. Transport other than Motor Lorries will follow Units on the march. Lorries will travel independently.

5. Units will march independently as follows:-

Unit.	Present Position.	Time.	Route.	Destination.
M.G.Battn.	TERNAS.	9.a.m.	AMBRINES	BEAUFORT.
16 Sussex.	FOUFFLIN RICAMETZ.	9.a.m.	TERNAS & AMBRINES.	MANIN.
12 Norfolks.	MAISNIL ST POL.	9.15.a.m.	TERNAS & AVERDOINGT	IZEL-les-HAMEAU.
10 Buffs.	BUNEVILLE.	9.30.a.m.	GOUY & AMBRINES.	- do -
230 Bde.H.Q.	- do -	9.40.a.m.	- do -	- do -
230 Fd.Amb.) L.T.M.B.)	MONTS EN TERNOIS.	10.15.a.m.	- do -	VILLERS-SIR-SIMON
15 Suffolks.	MAISNIL.	9.45.a.m.	TERNAS & AVERDOINGT.	PENIN.
R.M.R.E.	HOUVIN.	9.30.a.m.	BUNEVILLE-GOUY-AMBRINES.	GIVENCHY-le-NOBLE.
440 Coy. A.S.C.	FOUFFLIN.	10.30.a.m.	TERNAS & AVERDOINGT.	DOFFINE.

6. The Brigade Group must be in complete in the new area by 1.30.p.m.
   Units will immediately report their arrival to Bde,H.Q. at IZEL-les-HAMEAU.

7. Lorries will be available as follows:-

M.G.Battalion	3.	- 2
R.M.R.E.	1.	- 1
L.T.M.B. & Bde.H.Q.	1.	- 1
4 Battalions	2 lorries each.	2

no In addition to which 1 lorry will be shared by 10th Buffs and 15th Suffolks and 1 by 12th Norfolks and 16th Sussex.
   Guides for these lorries will report at Bde.H.Q. at 7.a.m. Suffolks and Sussex will send an extra guide each to Buffs and Norfolks respectively to take the extra lorries when half full to their own Units.

8. Bde.H.Q. will close in present site at 9.30.a.m. and will reopen on arrival at IZEL-les-HAMEAU.

9. ACKNOWLEDGE.

[signature]

Major,
Brigade Major.
230th Infantry Brigade.

Copies to:- No.1.74th Division
2.File.
3.10th Buffs.
4.12th Norfolks.
5.15th Suffolks.

SECRET. Copy No.3.

MEDICAL ARRANGEMENTS.

21st May 1918.

With reference to 74th Division Order No.59.

1. A Motor Ambulance with orderly and supply of dressings will be at entraining and detraining points during the move of the Division.

2. The D.A.D.M.S. Advanced Divisional Headquarters is arranging with D.D.M.S. Canadian Corps for evacuation of any cases pending arrival of Field Ambulances in the new area. He has been instructed to inform Brigades of arrangements.

3. The O.C.,229th Field Ambulance will deal with sick of 230th Brigade pending arrival of 230th Field Ambulance, and O.C. 230th Field Ambulance on arrival will deal with sick of 231st Brigade until arrival of 231st Field Ambulance.

4. ACKNOWLEDGE.

Lieut.Colonel,
A.D.M.S.
74th (Yeomanry) Division.

Copies to No.1. A.A.& Q.M.G.
2. H.Q.229th Infantry Brigade.
3. H.Q.230th Infantry Brigade.
4. H.Q.231st Infantry Brigade.
5. File.

B.M.S.364.

O.C. Buffs. M.G.Battn.
Norfolks. Bde,H.Q.
Suffolks. A.S.C.
Sussex. File.
L.T.M.B. R.M.R.E.

For information.

L Johnston

Major,
Brigade Major.
230th Infantry Brigade.

20th May 1918.

Army Form C. 2121
(in pads of 100).

"A" Form
MESSAGES AND SIGNALS.

No. of Message....................

Prefix..........Code..........m. Office of Origin and Service Instructions.	Words / Charge. Sent At..........m. To.......... By..........	This message is on a/c of OHM ....Service. [illegible] (Signature of "Franking Officer.")	Recd. at..........m. Date.......... From.......... By..........

TO { 230 Inf Bde

Sender's Number.	Day of Month.	In reply to Number.	AAA
* F72	20	Q66	

AM SENDING FOLLOWING TO
UNITS AT 5 PM TO-DAY
AAA. B.H.Q 2 GS WAGONS and
~~[illegible]~~
1 LIMBER – KENTS 4 GS NORFOLKS
4 SUFFOLKS 4 SUSSEX
4 MGB 4 AAA.

1 WAGON EACH FOR RMRE AND
FIELD AMBULANCE ARE JOINING
ME FROM 447 COMPANY
TO-MORROW AFTERNOON AAA
THEY WILL MEET UNITS AT
REFILLING POINT AT 5 PM

From 449 Coy ASC
Place
Time

The above may be forwarded as now corrected. (Z) [illegible] Captain

..........Censor. Signature of Addressor or person authorised to telegraph in his name

* This line should be erased if not required.

Wt. W492/M1647 100,000 pads. 4/17. W. & Co., Ltd. (E. 1187.) 449 Coy ASC

SECRET.

Reference ATTACHED ENTRAINING DETAILS.

The Divisional Train attached to Units will be entrained by Units as follows:-

Train No.	Wagons.	Horses.	Unit entraining.
10	3	6	(1 Wagon and 2 Horses from each of (Suffolks, Norfolks, Buffs.
11	3	6	Suffolks.
12	3	6	Norfolks.
13	3	6	Buffs.
14	3	6	Sussex.
15	1	2	Sussex.

Major,
Brigade Major.
230th Infantry Brigade.

30th May 1918.
Copies to:- Buffs. L.T.M.B.
Norfolks. M.G.Battn.
Suffolks. Bde.H.Q.
Sussex. A.S.C
File
RMRE

MOVE OF 74th (YEOMANRY) DIVISION, MAY 20TH.1918.

SECRET.

Entrain at RUE. & . . . . Consign to LIGNY ST.FLOCHEL.

Train No.	Marche.	Depart.	Date.	Contents.
10	T. @14	21.34	21/5/18.	230thBde.H.Q.- No.3 Sect.Signal Coy. * 1 Coy.Cooker & team of 10th E.Kents. * do do 12th Norfolks. * do do 15th Suffolks. Part of Divl.Train.
11	T. 18	1,34	22/5/18	* 15th Suffolks(less 1 Coy.Cooker & team 449th Coy.Divl.Trains Part of Divl.Train.
12	T. 22	5.34	"	* 12th Norfolks(less 1 Coy.Cooker & team 230th L.T.M.Bty.-Part of Divl.Train.
13	T. 2	9.34	"	* 10th E.Kents(less 1 Coy.Cooker & team) Part of Divl.Train.
14	T. 6	13.44	"	* 16th Sussex(less 1 Coy.Cooker & team) Part of Divl.Train.
15	T.10	17.44	"	5th R.W.F.- Part of Divl.Train. * 1 Coy.Cooker & team of 16th Sussex.
16	T,14	21.34	"	½ 74th M.G.Bn. & transport. 5th Signal Section - Part of Div.Train
17	T.18	1.34	23/5/18	½ 74th M.G.Bn.horses & transport.
18	T.22	5.34	"	231stBde,H.Q.- 230th Fd.Ambce. Part of Divl.Train. 4th Signal Section. 231st L.T.M.Bty. * 1 Coy.Cooker & team of 24th R.W.F.

When the sentence "Part of Divl.Train" occurs in the state it means the baggage and supply wagons attached from the Divl.Train to the Unit or Units proceeding by that train.

* Where "1 Coy.Cooker and team" appears, this should be read as "1 Coy.(i.e.10 Officers 250 O.R) 1 Field Cooker and 2 Horses". The requisite proportion of Battalion Transport will accompany this personnel, the remainder of Battalion Transport entraining with the Battalion.

Vol. 3.

Headquarters,
230th Inf. Bde.
(74th Division)

June 1918

VOLUME No.

BRITISH SALONIKA FORCE

WAR DIARY.

26th Division

VOL. No.	UNIT	PERIOD FROM	TO
27.	78th Machine Gun Company.	1.9.18	30.9.18
27.	79th do.	"	"

A.P. & S.D., Ska. 774/1070/1 2030 11/7/18 F&J.

169 Bde

August

1917

1. Hd Qrs 230th Inf Bde

Army Form C. 2118.

JUNE 18

Vol 3

230 INF BDE

BEF

Instructions regarding War Diaries and Intelligence Summaries are contained in F. S. Regs., Part II. and the Staff Manual respectively. Title pages will be prepared in manuscript.

WAR DIARY
or
~~INTELLIGENCE SUMMARY.~~
(Erase heading not required.)

JUNE 1918

Place	Date	Hour	Summary of Events and Information	Remarks and references to Appendices
IZEL-LES-HAMEAUX	1		B.G.C., B.M., Lt Col A.F. MORSE 12 Norfolks, & MAJOR BAXTON 10 BUFFS, umpired in a tactical scheme between 229th & 231st Inf Bdes.	
	2.		Mounted Officers taking part in Bde scheme tomorrow took part in a staff ride with the B.G.C.	
	3.		Bde scheme in which 10 Buffs & 16 Sussex with two sections of M.G. supported by 12th Norfolks and 2 Sects M.G. & L.T.M.B. attacked 15 Suffolks & 2 Sects M.G. – Insufficient room for employment & ... was encountered.	
	4	3pm	35 Officers from the Brigade attended lecture at AVESNE LE COMTE on TANKS by B.G.C. 1st TANK Bde.	
	5.		B.G.C. saw 10 Buffs in attack – B.M. attended 231st Inf Bde scheme.	
		PM	Competition in P. & B.T. on Sussex parade ground. Won by 16 Sussex, Suffolks 2nd, Norfolks 3rd. 10 Buffs could not compete owing to sickness.	
	6		B.G.C. inspected 15 Suffolks in the attack. –	
			B.M. called on O.C. Tanks and arranged for demonstration by tanks	
	7		Demonstration by Tanks on 229th Inf Bde parade ground at LIENCOURT given to 15 Suffolks & 16 Sussex attended by B.G.C. & B.M.	
	8		B.G.C. & S.C. watched 231st Inf Bde scheme	
		9am	8 Officers and 16 N.C.O.s from both Sussex and Buffs attended tank demonstration on 229 Bde parade ground at LIENCOURT.	[illegible] Brigade Major 230 Inf Bde –

(A7092). Wt. W12839/M1293. 750,000. 1/17. D. D. & L., Ltd. Forms/C.2118/14.

2 230 INF BDE B.E.F.

WAR DIARY

~~or~~

~~**INTELLIGENCE SUMMARY.**~~

(*Erase heading not required.*)

JUNE 1918

Army Form C. 2118.

Instructions regarding War Diaries and Intelligence Summaries are contained in F. S. Regs., Part II. and the Staff Manual respectively. Title pages will be prepared in manuscript.

Place	Date	Hour	Summary of Events and Information	Remarks and references to Appendices
IZEL-LES-HAMEAUX	9		Warning received to be ready to move in 9 hours warning instead of 24. Training confined to neighbourhood of billeting area.	
	10.		B.G.C. cancelled attack to be carried out by 12 Norfolks owing to rain. 10 Buffs and 16 Sussex went through poisonous gas.	
	11.		B.G.C. saw 12 Norfolks in the attack in training AREA. L.T.M.B. fired live rounds.	
	12		Training in billeting area.	
	13.		Representatives from each Bn watched Tank Demonstration at LIENCOURT	
		9 am	Staff ride under B.G.C.	
		3 pm	Attack and counter attack by 12 Norfolks and 15 Suffolks. 9 hours warning again extended to 24.	
	14	9.30 am	B.G.C's conference at Div HQrs discussed Bn transport & maintenance i.e. cutting down of extra men totally employed. B.G.C. & Bde and 25 officers from the Bde attended Demonstration by Mark V & Whippet Tanks at WAVRANS.	
	15		Divisional field day between 229th and 230th Inf Bdes – 230 Inf Bde attacked 229 Inf Bde holding position just South of BOIS DE FOSSE & BOIS ROBERMONT – 229th Inf Bde delivered counter attack. Suffolks supported by Buffs carried out primary attack.	J. Austin Major Bde Major 230 Inf Bde

3

Instructions regarding War Diaries and Intelligence Summaries are contained in F.S. Regs., Part. II. and the Staff Manual sespectively. Title pages will be prepared in manuscript.

230 INF BDE

BEF

WAR DIARY

or

~~INTELLIGENCE SUMMARY~~.

(Erase heading not required).

JUNE 1918

Army Form C. 2118.

Place	Date	Hour	Summary of Events and Information	Remarks and references to Appendices.
IZEL-LES-HAMEAUX	17	10am	BGC inspected 12 Norfolks –	
	17	2pm	BGC inspected 12 Norfolks in tactical exercise –	
	18		Practice attack carried out by two Coys 15th Suffolks in conjunction with 2 Sections TANKS against 1 Coy 16 Sussex 1 Sect M.G. An aeroplane cooperated with the attack – B.G.C. 1st Bde Tanks and L'Col [illegible] Tank Bn attended – Afterwards 1 Coy 12 Norfolks and 1 Coy 15th Suffolks each carried out an attack with Tanks	
	19		Bm. went to H.Q. 2nd Canadian Div to arrange attachment of each Bn 230 Inf Bde to 6th Canadian Bde in line for a two days tour. While there a wire came cancelling the same –	
	20	7pm	Received warning wire that 12 Norfolks together with 2/4 RWF and 12 RSF to leave 74 Div and form [illegible] Bde in 30th Division	
21st [illegible]		3pm	Demonstration with message carrying rockets at Bde HQ	
	22	10am	Demonstration by LTMB on range at GIVENCHY (1) of LTMB against isolated M.G. (2) LTMB barrage beginning at 280x and lifting to 350x, attended by COs and Coy Cmdrs BGC & BM –	
	23rd	7.30am	Received orders to be prepared to move early tomorrow.	
	24th	11am	Skeleton Signal Scheme with aeroplane –,	

[signature] Major, Bde Major 230 Inf Bde –

A.P. & S.D., Alex./$\frac{2009}{50025A}$/11 : 17/5M. W.M. & Co.

4.

Instructions regarding War Diaries and Intelligence Summaries are contained in F.S. Regs., Part. II. and the Staff Manual sespectively. Title pages will be prepared in manuscript.

230 INF BDE
BEF

WAR DIARY
or
~~INTELLIGENCE SUMMARY.~~
(Erase heading not required).

JUNE 1918

Army Form C. 2118.

Place	Date	Hour	Summary of Events and Information	Remarks and references to Appendices.
IZEL-LES-HAMEAUX	21st	12.30pm	Personnel of 12 Norfolks left by 12.30pm train from TINQUES station by tactical train together with personnel of 24 RWF and 12th RSF. Transport proceeded by Road –	
		11am	Demonstration of Tanks crushing wire carried out in a practice attack by 1 Coy 10 Buffs at LIENCOURT – Officers and NCOs of Buffs and Suffolks attended –	
	25		Received orders to move and entrain at LIGNY-ST FLOCHEL as follows:– B.H.Q., LTMB, 15 Suffolks, 16 Sussex, RMRE train to start at 10.10am. 16 Sussex, MG Bn, (joining this group) and F.AMB 14.10. Owing to orders not being delivered to BDE many immediately, first train did not start till 11am. as units arrived late. Most units had seven miles to march to the station, detrained AIRE 2.30pm and 5.30am with long march up to 8 miles to billet –	
			Units billetted as follows:– B.H.Q. 16 Sussex, FLECHIN, – 10 Buffs ENQUIN LES-MINES, – 15 Suffolks ERNY ST JULIEN – LTMB BOMCOURT – MG Bn LIGNY-LES-AIRES & WESTREHEM – F.AMB and RMRE FLECHINELLE.	
	26.		Training in billeting area. BM rode round looking for ranges –	
	27		Capt HE BLUNT left BHQ to report for duty to RFA. Capt DS CAMPBELL 10 Buffs reported to BHQ for duty as understudy.	[illegible] 230 Inf Bde

A.P. & S.D., Alex./ $\frac{2009}{50025A}$ /11 : 17/5M. W.M. & Co.

5

230 INF BDE

Instructions regarding War Diaries and Intelligence Summaries are contained in F.S. Regs., Part. II. and the Staff Manual sespectively. Title pages will be prepared in manuscript.

B.E.F.

WAR DIARY
or
INTELLIGENCE SUMMARY.
(Erase heading not required).

JUNE 1918

Army Form C. 2118.

Place	Date	Hour	Summary of Events and Information	Remarks and references to Appendices.
FLECHIN.	27	5.30pm	BM's Conference at Div HQ	
	28	—	Training ~~area~~ in billeting area	
	29	9am	BM. B.I.O. Bde Sig Officer. COs. Coy Cmdrs with runners and scouts from each Bn reconnoitred BUSNES & AMUSOIRES lines, conveyed there by lorries. Found lines in unfinished state, in many cases impossible to see over the corn.	
	29.		Received written orders for B.G. A.A. KENNEDY CMG from 75th Inf Bde to assume command of 230 Inf Bde vice B.G. W.J. BOWKER to report W.O.	
	30.		During early part of night 30/1st July considerable aeroplane activity heard with antiaircraft fire and some distant bombing. __Effective strength__ of units 10th Buffs 41 Officers 844 O.R. 15 Suffolks 39 " 924 " 16 Sussex 42 " 941 " L.T.M.B. 4 " 50 " __Health__ During latter part of month much influenza was noticed by troops, the large majority of men evacuated were suffering from this disease.	

I. Johnston Major
Bde Major
230 Inf Bde.

A.P. & S.D., Alex./$\frac{2009}{50025A}$/II: 17/5M. W.M. & Co.

Vol. 4.

Headquarters
230th Inf. Bde.
(74th Division)

July 1918.

BRITISH SALONIKA FORCE.

WAR DIARY.

27th Division.

VOL. NO.	UNIT	PERIOD FROM	TO
39.	C. R. E.	1-3-19	31-3-19
39	500th (Wessex) Field Co. R.E.	—	—
39	501st do do	—	—
39.	17th Field Coy. "	—	—
40.	Divisional Signal Coy. "	1-4-19	30-4-19

A.P. & S.D., Ska. 1118/1070/1 1000 14/1/19 Pap.

230 INF BDE

B.E.F.

Instructions regarding War Diaries and Intelligence Summaries are contained in F.S. Regs., Part. II. and the Staff Manual sespectively. Title pages will be prepared in manuscript.

WAR DIARY
or
~~INTELLIGENCE SUMMARY.~~
(Erase heading not required).

July 1918

Hd Qrs 230th Inf Bde

Army Form C. 2118.

Place	Date	Hour	Summary of Events and Information	Remarks and references to Appendices.
FLECHIN	July 1		Bde in G.H.Q. reserve.	4
		8.15am	Brig. Gen. W.J. BOWKER CMG DSO. left for England.	
		9.45am	Brig Gen A.A. KENNEDY CMG arrived and assumed Command	
		2pm	Brig Gen & B.M. saw 1 Coy of the Sussex doing wood fighting and then visited Col JARVIS 15th Suffolks & Major BAIRSTOW 10th Buffs.	
	2		B.G.C. B.M. B.I.O. & Bde Sig Officer. O.C. Bns, Coy. Cmdrs and one other officer per Bn with runners carried out reconnaissance of parts of BUSNES - STEENBECQUE and AMUSOIRE - HAVERSKIERQUE - LAMBOTTE lines.	
			The front line of this sector held by 5th Division.	
	3		B.G.C. attended Battn scheme carried out by 15th Suffolks.	
	4		Same parties as before reconnoitred line of left Bde of Right Div i.e. from LABEUVRIERE (exc) to PONT DE REVEILLON, found line in good condition but nothing to mark R.A.P.s B.H.Q. etc. - The line in front of reconnoitred line is held by 3rd Div.	
			B.G.C. called on MAJOR GENERAL DEVERELLE 3rd Div at CHAT. LABEUVRIERE	
	5		Reconnaissance carried out by same parties less B.M. of Left Div Sector from PONT DE REVEILLON to BUSNES (exc) - O.C. 7th [illegible] attended	

[illegible] Maj.
Brig Maj. 230 Inf Bde

A.P. & S.D., Alex./$\frac{2009}{50025A}$/II : 17/5M. W.M. & Co.

2.

230 INF. BDE

BEF

Instructions regarding War Diaries and Intelligence Summaries are contained in F.S. Regs., Part. II. and the Staff Manual sespectively. Title pages will be prepared in manuscript.

WAR DIARY

~~or~~

~~INTELLIGENCE SUMMARY.~~

~~(Erase heading not required).~~

JULY 1918

Army Form C. 2118.

Place	Date	Hour	Summary of Events and Information	Remarks and references to Appendices.
FLECHIN	July 5th	11 AM.	BGC attended conference at Divisional H.Qrs to meet Corps Commander and carried out reconnaissance afterwards.	
	6.		BGC with G.O.C. Div & BGCs 229 & 231 Inf Bdes carried out reconnaissance of HINGES - MT BERNENCHON RIDGE with a view to making counter attack on MT BERNENCHON from S.W. direction in the event of it being captured by the enemy.	
			Inter battalion scheme between 10 Buffs and 16 Sussex - 10 Buffs attacked 16 Sussex from Northerly direction and drove them back through CUHEM to BOMY WOOD. 10 Buffs had 1½ sections M.G. Bn attached also 1 Batty RFA. Each battalion had 1 sect LTMB attached.	
	7		DAQMG called.	
	/8	AM	BGC visited Buffs training and inspected Buffs & Sussex transport in the morning.	
			BM left for U.K. on leave.	
			Warning order to relieve 61st Div in the line on July 10th.	
			Instructions for advanced parties received from Division.	
	9	9 AM	BGC left to visit H.Qrs 182nd Inf Bde re taking over line.	
			Instructions for Advanced parties issued to units.	
			Div order for relief received.	
	10.		Bde orders No 41 issued for relief of 182 I.B. units moved to forward area by bus - Buffs at 9am transport 9.30 am	

[illegible] Major
BM 230 Inf Bde

A.P. & S.D., Alex./2009/50025A/II : 17/5M. W.M. & Co.

3.

230 Inf Bde.

WAR DIARY
~~or~~
~~INTELLIGENCE SUMMARY.~~
~~(Erase heading not required).~~

July 1918

BEF

Army Form C. 2118.

Instructions regarding War Diaries and Intelligence Summaries are contained in F.S. Regs., Part. II. and the Staff Manual sespectively. Title pages will be prepared in manuscript.

Place	Date	Hour	Summary of Events and Information	Remarks and references to Appendices.
FLECHIN	July 10		Bde H.Qrs 10AM Transport at 10.20 AM at Ham.en.Artois.	
			15 Suffolks 3pm " 11 Am	
			16 Sussex 4pm " 10.30 Am	
			All units reported in new area at 7.45pm - BGC and Staff Capt visited 182 I.B. advance H.Q. GSO I 74 Div visited B.H.Q.	
			Orders for Bde as Reserve to 61st Div issued.	
	11.		Relief of 182 Inf Bde. BGC went round line.	
		5pm	229 Inf Bde took over Bde H.Q. at Ham.en.Artois	
			TMB completed relief at 7.50pm. - Buffs at 10.30pm.	
			Bde H.Qrs moved to right Section H.Qrs. P31.c3.7.	
	12.	1.10am	15th Suffolks relief complete at 1.10am. 16 Sussex at 3.am.	
			Relief reported to 61st and 74th Divisions.	
			GSO 2 74 Div called.	
		10Am	RMRE relieved at 10AM.-	
			Casualties 1 O.R. Killed 16 Sussex.	
	13.	10.30Am	C.R.E called - New Southern boundary received from the 61 Div	
			BGC visited line with I.O.	
			Interpreter Pte HENIN reported for duty.	
			Casualties 1 OR wounded 16 Sussex	
	14.	10AM	G.O.C. visited Bde H.Q. 10.10AM.	
		3pm	BGC met COs. OCRE and 2nd i/c MG Coy at 3pm P23 a 3.4	
		10AM	GOC 74 Div took command of Sector from 61st Div	[illegible] Major [illegible] 230 Inf Bde

A.P. & S.D., Alex./2009/50025A/11: 17/5M. W.M. & Co.

4.

230 Inf Bde

WAR DIARY
or
~~INTELLIGENCE SUMMARY.~~

(~~Erase heading not required.~~)

Army Form C. 2118.

Instructions regarding War Diaries and Intelligence Summaries are contained in F. S. Regs., Part II. and the Staff Manual respectively. Title pages will be prepared in manuscript.

BEF

Place	Date	Hour	Summary of Events and Information	Remarks and references to Appendices
CHATEAU BEAULIEU	JULY 15	5/pm	BGC and of BM attended conference at the Division	
			Capt G CHIPPER 1st N.F reported as acting Bde Major.	
	16.	9.30am	OC. RFA Bde M.G. Coy Cmdr and OC LTMB conference at B.HQ.	
		12.20am	Vicinity of BHQ. shelled about 12.20 am no damage.	
	17.		Night 16/17 wet and thundery Order No 44 (attached) issued	Order No 44 APP "A"
			10th Buffs had 2 OR killed and 7 OR wounded by shell when working	
			on AMWOIRE Switch, reported to have been one of our shells.	
	18.		Weather fair. Army Commander visited Bde HQrs. and Reserve line	
			accompanied by Divisional Cmdr.	
	19.	AM.	Occasional light showers - Div Cmdr called during the morning.	
		PM.	BGGS, GOC RA and DAQMG XI Corps called in the afternoon.	
	20.		Orders No 45 & 46 ~~attached~~ issued	
			B.G. Hoare went round line with BGC	~~Order No 45~~
	21		Fine windy day - fine moonlight night Raid on Q8C 88 12 midnight	
			by 16 Sussex 1 off & 20 OR - successful. 3 prisoners 10 of 102 RIR	
			23rd Reserve Div (Saxon), normal. Our casualties two wounded. [illegible]	
	22.		Fine day - BGGS and DAQMG XI Corps called ~~Order 46 attached~~ also GOC 3rd Div	Order No 46 APP B
			OC. 7th [illegible] Bn called.	
			H.V. Gun active on road between 11/pm and midnight	
	23.		Heavy rain night 22/23	
			Bde relieved in line by 229 Inf Bde see order No 45 attached	Order No 45 APP. C
			Casualties during relief 8 OR wounded in 16 Sussex one of which died of wounds	

[illegible] Major
Brigade Major 230 Inf Bde.

D. D. & L., London, E.C. (A8001) Wt. W1771/M2031 750,000 5/17 Sch. 52 Forms/C2118/14

5

230 INF. BDE

Instructions regarding War Diaries and Intelligence Summaries are contained in F. S. Regs., Part II. and the Staff Manual respectively. Title pages will be prepared in manuscript.

BEF

WAR DIARY
or
INTELLIGENCE SUMMARY.
(Erase heading not required.)

JULY 1918

Army Form C. 2118.

Place	Date	Hour	Summary of Events and Information	Remarks and references to Appendices
HAM-EN-ARTOIS	JULY 24		Relief complete 4 am.	
			BDE moved into new area	
			BHQ ~~to~~ 15 Suffks. LTMB to HAM-EN-ARTOIS.	
			10 Buffs to MIQUELLERIE	
			16 Sussex to GUARBECQUE.	
			During the tour in the trenches the following casualties occurred 1 Officer wounded, 4 O.R. Killed, 32 O.R. wounded.	
		3pm ~~1500~~	Bde Major returned from leave.	
	25		BGC & BM reconnoitred approaches to part of Div' line N. of SIVENANT and bridges over CANAL DE LA LYS.	
		2pm	Capt C. CHIPPER left for 3rd Division.	
			Some showers during the day.	
		3.30pm	Conference of Bn Comdrs and O.C. LTMB.	
	26.		Heavy rain during the night	
		1130 Am	BGRA called. GSO 2 XI also called.	
	27.		Rained during night 26/27th and on and off all day 27th.	
			Corps Horse show at ROCQUETOIRE attended by BGC and 1 lorry load from each Bn.	
			BM went to 8th Bde H.Q. for 4 days instruction in the line.	
	28.		Fine day BGC visited 10 Buffs in the afternoon.	

[signature] Major
Bde Major 230 Inf Bde

D. D. & L., London, E.C.
(A8004) Wt. W1771/M2031 750,000 5/17 Sch. 52 Forms/C2118/14

6.

230 INF BDE

Instructions regarding War Diaries and Intelligence Summaries are contained in F. S. Regs., Part II. and the Staff Manual respectively. Title pages will be prepared in manuscript.

BEF

WAR DIARY

~~or~~

~~INTELLIGENCE SUMMARY.~~

(~~Erase heading not required.~~)

JULY 1918

Army Form C. 2118.

Place	Date	Hour	Summary of Events and Information	Remarks and references to Appendices
HAM-EN-ARTOIS	JULY 29		Fine weather - Lt Col STACEY 1st AUST. Div lectured to 15th Suffks in the afternoon on Trench Raids - BGC attended - G.O.C. called.	
	30		Lt Col STACY lectured to 16 Sussex in morning and 10th Buffs in the afternoon on Trench Raids.	
	31.		Fine weather - BGC carried out Tactical Exercise without troops Cos, 2nd in C, and Adjts - C. Coy Cmds M.G. Bn - Exercise consisted of moving to position of assembly, and then for contingency "B" (move Eastwards) in Defence scheme.	
			BM. returned from 8th Bde -	
			Health of the troops during the month has much improved & is now good -	
			Effective strength of units	
			10th Buffs. 40 officers 876 OR	
			15 Suffks 39 " 960 "	
			16 Sussex 38 " 900 "	
			LTMB. 4 " 50 "	
			[illegible] Major Bde Major 230 Inf Bde.	

D. D. & L., London, E.C.
(A8004) Wt. W1771/M2031 750,000 5/17 Sch. 52 Forms/C2118/14

S E C R E T.

Copy No.....11.....

230th INFANTRY BRIGADE ORDER No 41.

Reference Map:- 36a. (1:40,000). 10-7-18.

1. The 74th Division is relieving the 61st Division in the front system commencing the night of the 10th/11th inst. Relief will be completed by 3 a.m. on 14th inst.

2. The Brigade is now in Divisional Reserve (61st Division) until 4 p.m. 11th inst.

3. It will relieve the 182nd Infantry Brigade in the ROBECQ Section on the 11th and night of 11th/12th inst. as detailed in attached Table.

4. All documents, maps in connection with the section, aeroplane photos, S.O.S. grenades, trench and billet stores will be taken over from outgoing Units and receipts given.

5. All details of relief not dealt with in these Orders will be arranged direct between Commanding Officers concerned.

6. Guides from the advanced parties, which proceeded to the ROBECQ Section on the 9th inst., are to be detailed to conduct Companies from their billets to their locations in the Section.

7. Right Group machine guns are being relieved on night 12th/13th under arrangements being made by O.C., 74th Bn. M.G.Corps.

8. Command of the ROBECQ Section will pass to G.O.C., 230th Infantry Brigade on completion of relief (infantry portion) night of 11th/12th.

9. Brigade Headquarters will close at HAM-en-ARTOIS at 5 p.m. on 11th inst and open at CHATEAU de BEAULIEU (P.31.c.3.7.) at same hour.

Percy Cockerill

Capt,
for Brigade Major,
230th Infantry Brigade.

Issued at

Copies to :-

No.1. File.	8. 182nd Inf.Bde.
2. C.O.,Buffs.	9. 74th M.G.Battn.
3. Suffolks.	10. 231st Inf.Bde.
4. Sussex.	11. War Diary.
5. L.T.M.B.	12. " "
6. R.M.R.E.	13. 229th Inf.Bde.
7. Fld.Ambce.	14. Staff Capt.
	15. 74 Division

S E C R E T.

RELIEF TABLE ISSUED WITH 230th INFANTRY BRIGADE ORDER No. 41. dated 10-7-18.

Serial No.	U N I T,	From	To relieve	Location.	REMARKS.
1.	15th Suffolks.	LA MIQUELLERIE.	2/8 Worcesters.	Right Sub-section. (H.Q.,P.24.d.75.80.)	Not to cross the AIRE-LA BASSEE Canal before 9-30 p.m.
2.	16th Sussex.	GUARBECQUE.	2/7 Warwicks.	Left Sub-section. (H.Q.,P.17.b.10.25.)	- do -
3.	10th Buffs.	HAM-on-ARTOIS.	2/6 Warwicks.	LA PIERRIERE. (in Brigade Reserve).	Not to reach LA PIERRIERE before 9-30 p.m.
4.	230th L.T.M.B.	HAM-on-ARTOIS.	182 L.T.M.B.	4 guns in line.	Relief to be complete by 8 p.m.

NOTE. When moving forward in relief distances of 100 yards to be preserved between Companies.

BMA/2
10.7.18.

HEADQUARTERS 230th INFANTRY BRIGADE

No. BMA/2

Date 10.7.18.

S E C R E T.

Copy No. 11

230th INFANTRY BRIGADE ORDER No.43.

Reference Map Sheet [illegible] (1/40,000)

10th July 1918.

1. On receipt of Orders to "Man Battle Stations" the Brigade will act as follows while in Divisional Reserve :-

(a) Brigade Headquarters move up to the Headquarters of the left advanced Brigade in O.17.d.

(b) The 3 Battalions move from present billets to positions of assembly as under :-

(i) Suffolks.(LA MIQUELLERIE) to O.24.a.

(ii) Sussex.(GUARBECQUE) to P.17.c. North of the Canal and West of the Railway.

(iii) Buffs. (HAM-EN-ARTOIS) to O.18.a.

(c) One Company of the Machine Gun Battalion also joins the Brigade and has its position of assembly in O.19.a.

2. Units must be prepared to concentrate at the above positions of assembly at short notice and to move therefrom fully equipped for action. Dispersed formations should be adopted to minimise risk of casualty from shell fire.

3. The Brigade is to be prepared to move:-

(a) Counter attack to regain any portion of the Divisional front system - general line [illegible].30.c.central to Q.1. central. Such counter attack would be carried out from a forward assembly position in the AMUSOIRES - HAVERSKERQUE line.

(b) Form a defensive line on the South along the General line of the N O C River - in the event of the enemy penetrating our front further South and seizing the HINGES - MT BERNENCHON Ridge.

(c) Counter attack along the North side of the LYS CANAL, in event of the Division on our left being driven back, while our own Divisional front remained intact.

/2

4. When Units move out to their positions of assembly all transport, less pack mules, is to be sent back to HAM-EN-ARTOIS where it will come under the orders of the Brigade Transport Officer.

Acknowledge

Percy Cockerill
Capt,
for Brigade Major.
230th Infantry Brigade.

Issued at 11 pm

Copies to:-

No.1. Buffs.
2. 15th Suffolks.
3. 16th Sussex.
4. 74th M.G.Battalion.
5. O.C., No.[illegible] Signal Section.
6. 61st Division.
7. 74th Division.
8. 231st Brigade.
9. Staff Capt.
10. War Diary.
11. File.
12. Bde Transport Officer

APP A

Copy No 3.

Not to be taken forward
of Battalion Headquarters.

S E C R E T.

230th INFANTRY BRIGADE ORDER No.44

17-7-18.

1. The following alteration in allotment of troops in the front system will come into force from the night of the 18/19 instant, and the necessary alterations will be made in all defence schemes.
The right Battalion in the ROBECQ sector will be disposed with one Company in the front and support lines - two Companies in the reserve line and one Company in the HAVERSKERQUE - AMUSOIRES line.
The left Battalion will remain disposed as at present, viz., with two Companies in the front and support lines - 1 Company in the Reserve line and one Company in the HAVERSKERQUE - AMUSOIRES line.

2. The inter-battalion boundary will be Q.14 central, thence by the road past BERKSHIRE FARM in Q.14.c.central to Q.14.c.0.3. inclusive to the left Battalion - thence W.N.W. to the Reserve line in Q.13.c.4.8. - thence S.W. to the point where the HAVERSKERQUE - AMUSOIRES line crosses the road at P.24.c.3.6. - (road inclusive to the right Battalion) - thence as at present.

3. A suitable site is to be selected by O.C., Right Battalion, North of the ROBECQ - BERKSHIRE FARM road and West of the Reserve Line, for the H.Q. of the extra Company of the Right Battalion which is to be accommodated in the Reserve Line, and construction proceeded with forthwith.

4. A site has been approved for a new Right Battalion H.Q., in an orchard North of the ROBECQ - BERKSHIRE FARM Road, about P.23.d.8.5. The construction of these H.Q., is to be commenced forthwith.

5. The Companies in the HAVERSKERQUE - AMUSOIRES line, less one platoon, or its equivalent made up of Lewis Gunners of each Company, are at the disposal of Battalion Commanders in forward system for carrying up material and for work as desired in any portion of their sectors at night.

6. PRIORITY OF WORK.

NOTE. Work on the Reserve line is carried out under Divisional Orders and the garrison of that line cannot be detailed for work elsewhere.
Battalion Commanders will give precedence in alloting working parties to the following in order of importance.

(a) Parties, strength up to the number of tools available, to cut the crops on either side of the wire to a width of about 20 feet inside and 15 feet outside in both the Support and HAVERSKERQUE - AMUSOIRES lines.
The garrisons of machine gun posts are available to assist in this in the vicinity of their posts, and where possible the work should be continued also during the day.

App

D

(b) i. Making a continuous (less occasional overlapping narrow gaps for passage of troops to the front) breastwork along the support line to facilitate communication laterally.
ii. Construction of defended localities in the support line, tactically sited for flank defence. The strong point on the right of the Right Battalion Support line, site of which has been selected by the Brigadier in conjunction with O.C., Right Battalion, is to be given precedence of work in this connection in the Right Battalion Sector.

(c) Construction of shelters for infantry and artillery garrisons in the several lines.

(d) Siting of a communication trench per Battalion sector, to connect all systems. Pending construction, the site of these will in the first place be marked by screens, after the site has been approved.

(e) Improvement of existing wire where required. Cutting and marking of gaps in wire across tracks leading from the HAVERSKERQUE - AMUSOIRES line to the Reserve and Support lines. Wire should be made to overlap at the gaps.

NOTE. Work on the H.Q., mentioned in paras 3 & 4 is to be carried out simultaneously with the foregoing.

C. Clifton Capt,
a/Brigade Major.
230th Infantry Brigade.

Issued at

Copies to:-
No.1. File.
2. "
3. War Diary.
4. O.C.Buffs.
5. Suffolks.
6. Sussex.
7. R.M.R.F.

MESSAGES AND SIGNALS. No. of Message ....

Prefix ...... Code ...... m. Office of Origin and Service Instructions.	Words. Charge.	This message is on a/c of:	Recd. at ...... m.
DRLS	Sent At ...... m. To ...... By	...... Service. SECRET (Signature of "Franking Officer.")	Date ...... From ...... By ......

TO 16th Sussex 230 LTM By 231
RA Corps ark 74th Div Inf Bde
R Cy 74 M.G Bn 15th Suff.

Sender's Number.	Day of Month.	In reply to Number.	AAA
* G 31	21		

Ref 230 Inf Bde Order No 46

Zero hour 12 midnight

From 230 Inf Bde
Place
Time

The above may be forwarded as now corrected. ...... *Censor.*

(Z) C. Clifton Capt
Signature of Addressor or person authorised to telegraph in his name.

* This line, except **AAA**, should be erased if not required.

Wt. W 3253/P511. 500,000 Pads. 1/18. B. & S. Ltd. **(E2389.)**

SECRET.

Copy No. 1

230th INFANTRY BRIGADE ORDER No. 46.

Ref. Sheet 36A S.E.
Edn. 8A 1/20,000

20th July 1918.

1. RAID. On the night July 21st/22nd 16th Sussex (Yeo) Regt will carry out a raid on enemy's line about Q.8.c.8.8 with artillery co-operation.

2. OBJECT. To obtain prisoners and identifications and to harass the enemy.

3. STRENGTH. 1 Officer and 20 Other Ranks.

4. PROGRAMME.

Zero	Artillery bombardment of enemy's front line starts. Raiding party in position 100 yards from enemy's wire start crawling forward as far as possible.
Zero + 1 minute	Artillery lift over, leaving a box barrage. Party advance to a point fixed by reconnaissance just South of Q.8.c.8.8 and cut their way through enemy's wire.
Zero + 2 minutes	Party get through enemy's wire and work North up enemy's posts.
Zero + 12 minutes	Party return through enemy's wire.
Zero + 17 minutes	Artillery fire ceases.

5. MACHINE GUNS.
'B' Coy 74th M.G.Battn will co-operate with artillery by fire on flanks of portion of line attacked.

6. TRENCH MORTARS.
230th Light Trench Mortar Battery will create a diversion by firing bursts on road Q.14.a.6.2 to Q.14.a.7.8 and on road junction Q.14.d.4.9

7. SYNCHRONISATION OF WATCHES. An Officer from 16th Sussex, Right Group Artillery, 'B' Coy 74th M.G.Battn and 230th L.T.M.Battery will synchronise watches with a representative of Brigade Headquarters at Left Battalion Headquarters P.17.b.20.75 at 6.30 p.m.

8. ZERO HOUR will be notified later.

9. ACKNOWLEDGE.

C. Chipper
Captain,
a/Brigade Major,
230th Infantry Brigade.

Issued at 5.30 pm by DR.

Copy No, 1 File
2 16th Sussex
3 Right Group Artillery
4 'B' Coy 74th M.G.Bn.
5 230th L.T.M.Battery
6 74th Division
7 15th Suffolks) for information.
8 231st Inf.Bde)
9)
10) War Diary.

SECRET. app A Copy No. 1...

am

230th INFANTRY BRIGADE ORDER No.45

Ref.Map. 36A. 20-7-18

1. The 229th Infantry Brigade now in Divisional Reserve is relieving the Brigade in the ROBECQ Section on the night of 23rd/24th as detailed in attached Table.

2. All documents, maps in connection with the Section, aeroplane photos, work tables, S.O.S. grenades, trench and billet stores will be handed over to relieving Units and receipts obtained.

3. Further details of relief not dealt with in these Orders will be arranged direct between C.O's concerned, including the accommodation of advanced parties of 229th Brigade arriving night of 21st/22nd.

4. To assist the 229th Brigade to become familiar with the Section the following will remain behind to be attached to Units in the Line for a further 24 hours:-

Bde.H.Q.	Intelligence Officer and 3 O.R. Signal Section.
With each Battalion in the Line	1 Officer, 2 N.C.O's with Battn.H.Q.
	2 N.C.O's with each Coy.

5. On relief by the 229th Brigade the 230th Brigade will come into Divisional Reserve. Attention is directed to Extracts from Defence Scheme,"Instructions for Brigade in Divisional Reserve" issued herewith to Battalions.
The reconnaissances (a) (b) and (c) enumerated in para 3 will be carried out as soon as Officers and N.C.O's become available.
All Units must be able to provide guides to conduct them to their preliminary assembly positions mentioned in para 6 (b) and thence by day or night to the assembly positions (a).
The task of providing guides by day or night for contingency (b) is allotted to the 10th Buffs and that for (c) to the 16th Sussex.

6. Command of the ROBECQ Section will pass to G.O.C.,229th Infantry Brigade at 9 a.m. on 24th.

7. Bde.H.Q. will close at CHATEAU DE BEAULIEU at 9 a.m. on 24th instant and open at HAM-en-ARTOIS at same hour.

9 ACKNOWLEDGE

8. Completion of relief will be notified to these headquarters by wiring the word ACE.

C. Chipper Capt,
A/Brigade Major.
230th Infantry Brigade.

Issued at 7.35 pm

Copies to:-

No.1.File.	No.8. 229th Inf.Bde.
2.O.C.Buffs.	9. 231st Inf.Bde.
3. Suffolks.	10. 12th Inf.Bde.
4. Sussex.	11. 74th Division.
5. L.T.M.B.	12. 74th M.G.Battn.
6. R.M.R.E.	13. Staff Capt.
7. Fd.Ambce.	14. War Diary.
	15. " "
	16. B.T.O.
	17. Bde. Sig. Ofr.
	18 Bde. Supply Ofr.

Bridge guards will be relieved by units of 229 Bde by 4 pm. on 23rd.

S E C R E T.

RELIEF TABLE issued with 230th INFANTRY BRIGADE ORDER No.45. dated 20/7/18

Serial No.	Unit.	Location.	Relieved by	On relief to
1.	15th Suffolks.	Right Sub-section (H.Q.,I.24.d.75.80.)	12th Somerset Light Inf.	HAM-EN-ARTOIS
2.	16th Sussex.	Left Sub-section (H.Q.,P.17.b.10.25.)	16th Devons.	GUARBECQUE.
3.	10th Buffs.	LA PIERRIERE. (in Brigade Reserve).	14th Black Watch.	LA MIQUELLERIE.
4.	230th L.T.M.B.		229th L.T.M.B.	HAM-EN-ARTOIS.

NOTE. When moving out on relief, distances of 100 yards to be preserved between platoons.

SECRET

EXTRACTS FROM DEFENCE SCHEME

Appended to 250th Inf.Bde. Order No.45. dated 20-7-18.

---

3. The Brigade in Divisional Reserve will be prepared to:-

(a) Counter attack deliberately to regain any part of the Line of Retention captured by the enemy.

(b) In the event of a successful attack against the Division on our Right.

(i) Form a flank South of the NOC River and East of MARQUOIS.

(ii) Counter attack North of LA BASSEE Canal and towards RIEZ du VINAGE.

(c) In the event of a successful attack against the Division on our left.

(i) Form a flank from the ST FLORIS Switbh to the HAVERSKERQUE-le-SART Road.in J.29.c.

(ii) Counter attack towards CORBIE and LA MOTTE BAUDET.

In accordance with the above, the Brigade in Divisional Reserve will reconnoitre, both by day and night,

(a) Lines of advance from positions of assembly to the AMUSOIRES-HAVERSKERQUE line - which will be the assembly position from which any counter attack for the recapture of any portion of our Front System will be launched.

(b) Lines of advance North of LA BASSEE Canal from positions of assembly to the line of the NOC River.

(c) Lines of advance from positions of assembly - North of the COURANT BRAYELLE - across the bridges over the LYS N. of ST VENANT.

6. On receipt of Order"Man Battle Stations"

(b) H.Q.,Infantry Brigade in Divisional Reserve will move to H.Q. of Brigade holding ST FLORIS Section (P.7.c.)

1 battalion from LA MIQUELLERIE will move to assembly position in the vicinity of O.24.a.

1 battalion from GUARBECQUE will move to assembly position in vicinity of P.13.a. North of the Canal and West of the Railway.

1 battalion from HAM-EN-ARTOIS will move to assembly position in vicinity of O.18.a.

Secret   Copy No 11

ADMINISTRATIVE ORDERS

Relative to 230th Infantry Brigade Order No.45 of 20-7-18.

Ref.Sheet. No.36A.   22-7-18.

1. BATHS.

		HAM-EN-ARTOIS	GUARBECQUE
23-7-18	10th Buffs. 8 a.m.- 7 p.m.	-	500
24-7-18	15th Suffolks. 9 a.m.- 7 p.m.	700	-
	16th Sussex. 9 a.m.- 7 p.m.	-	500
25-7-18	15th Suffolks. 8 a.m.- 10 a.m.	To complete.	-
	L.T.M.B.) 10 a.m.- Bde.H.Q.) 12 noon.	160	
	10th Buffs. 2 p.m.- 4 p.m.	To complete.	
	16th Sussex. 8 a.m.- 3 p.m.	-	To complete.

Following parties will be detailed to work to complete the Baths, they should assume their duties one hour before the first Unit is due to commence bathing.

23-7-28	GUARBECQUE	10th Buffs.	1 Cpl.	2 men.
24-7-18) 25-7-18)	do	16th Sussex.	1 "	2 "
24-7-18) 25-7-18)	HAM EN ARTOIS	15th Suffolks.	1 "	2 "

2. "B" Teams.
"B" Teams will rejoin their Units in the Reserve Bde Area on the 23rd July. They will act as advance billeting parties. One Motor Lorry will be allotted to the "B" Teams of each Battalion for the conveyance of Blankets from WITTERNESSE.

3. BAGGAGE WAGONS.
Baggage wagons will report to Units' Transport Lines on the 23rd by 10 a.m. for the conveyance of kits to the new area. They will rejoin 449 Coy A.S.C. the same day.

4. RATIONS.
Rations drawn on 23rd for consumption 24th will be delivered by 449 Coy A.S.C. to the new area. Q.M's will arrange to off load there.
Refilling point will remain as at present.

5. REGIMENTAL EQUIPMENT S.A.A.
Units will arrange to exchange ~~20~~4 full boxes of S.A.A. with their opposite numbers.

6. <u>TRENCH STORES, AMMUNITION DUMPS, etc.</u>
Units will hand over all Trench and Area Stores and Ammunition Reserve Ration and Water Dumps, and obtain a receipt on the pro-forma already issued.
Those Lists will be forwarded to Brigade Headquarters by 4 p.m. 24th inst.nt.

Percy h Cockerill
Capt,
Staff Capt.
230th Infantry Brigade.

Issued at

Copies to:-

No. 1. O.C.Buffs.
2. Suffolks.
3. Sussex.
4. L.T.M.B.
5. Bde.Supply Officer.

No.6. O.C. 449 Train Coy.
7. "B" Teams.
8. R.M.R.E.
9. Fd.Ambce.
10. File.
11. Brigade Major.

L I S T of PAPERS handed over to 229th Inf.Bde 24/7/18.

1. 61st DIVISION Files.

'A' A.A Defence, Gas, Machine Guns, Defence Schemes, Action in case of attack.

'B' Trench File, Work Policy File, Raids.

'C' Signalling, Artillery, Trench Mortars.

'D' Bridges & Bridge Demolitions, Road Mines, Provost Arrangements, S.O.S. Signals, Various.

2. Extract from Minutes of Conference at Division July 15/18.
Subject:- "WORK"

3. Work Table - ROBECQ SECTOR - 2 copies.

4. 230th Brigade Defence Scheme & Maps shewing area, posts and H.Q.

5. Proposed sites for communication trenches and screened approaches (with Division for approval).

6. Sketches shewing positions of L.T.Mortars and Dumps.

7. Correspondence re 4th Div. 6" T.M's in our area.

8. Group Orders - Right Group Artillery - re S.O.S.

9. Location State - Right Flank Brigade.

10. Medical Arrangements, ROBECQ SECTOR, and Dumps.

Handed over by:-

Taken over by:- A.J.W. Tuck Captain Brigade Major 229 Inf Bde 23.7.18.

S E C R E T.

RELIEF TABLE issued with 230th INFANTRY BRIGADE ORDER No.45. dated 20/7/18

Serial No.	Unit.	Location.	Relieved by	On relief to
1.	15th Suffolks.	Right Sub-section (H.Q., P.24.d.75.80.)	12th Somerset Light Inf.	HAM-EN-ARTOIS
2.	16th Sussex.	Left Sub-section. (H.Q., P.17.b.10.25.)	16th Devons.	GUARBECQUE.
3.	10th Buffs.	LA PIERRIERE. (in Brigade Reserve).	14th Black Watch.	LA MIQUELLERIE.
4.	230th L.T.M.B.		229th L.T.M.B.	HAM-EN-ARTOIS.

NOTE. When moving out on relief, distances of 100 yards to be preserved between platoons.

SECRET. App "C"   Copy No. 14...

230th INFANTRY BRIGADE ORDER No.45

Ref.Map. 36A.   20-7-18

1. The 229th Infantry Brigade now in Divisional Reserve is relieving the Brigade in the ROBECQ Section on the night of 23rd/24th as detailed in attached Table.

2. All documents, maps in connection with the Section, aeroplane photos, work tables, S.O.S. grenades, trench and billet stores will be handed over to relieving Units and receipts obtained.

3. Further details of relief not dealt with in these Orders will be arranged direct between C.O's concerned, including the accommodation of advanced parties of 229th Brigade arriving night of 21st/22nd.

4. To assist the 229th Brigade to become familiar with the Section the following will remain behind to be attached to Units in the Line for a further 24 hours:-

   Bde.H.Q. — Intelligence Officer and 3 O.R. Signal Section.

   With each Battalion in the Line — 1 Officer, 2 N.C.O's with Battn.H.Q.
   2 N.C.O's with each Coy.

5. On relief by the 229th Brigade the 230th Brigade will come into Divisional Reserve. Attention is directed to Extracts from Defence Scheme,"Instructions for Brigade in Divisional Reserve" issued herewith to Battalions.
The reconnaissances (a) (b) and (c) enumerated in para 3 will be carried out as soon as Officers and N.C.O's become available.
All Units must be able to provide guides to conduct them to their preliminary assembly positions mentioned in para 6 (b) and thence by day or night to the assembly positions (a)
The task of providing guides by day or night for contingency (b) is allotted to the 10th Buffs and that for (c) to the 16th Sussex.

6. Command of the ROBECQ Section will pass to G.O.C., 229th Infantry Brigade at 9 a.m. on 24th.

7. Bde.H.Q. will close at CHATEAU DE BEAULIEU at 9 a.m. on 24th instant and open at HAM-en-ARTOIS at same hour.

8 ACKNOWLEDGE

C. Chipper Capt,
A/Brigade Major.
230th Infantry Brigade.

Issued at

Copies to:-

No.1. File.	No.8. 229th Inf.Bde.
2. O.C. Buffs.	9. 231st Inf.Bde.
3. Suffolks.	10. 12th Inf.Bde.
4. Sussex.	11. 74th Division.
5. L.T.M.B.	12. 74th M.G.Battn.
6. R.M.R.E.	13. Staff Capt.
7. Fd.Ambce.	14. War Diary.
	15. " "

App C

APP B

SECRET.

Copy No. 10

230th INFANTRY BRIGADE ORDER No. 43.

Ref.Sheet 36A S.E.
Edn.8A 1/20,000

20th July 1918.

1. RAID. On the night July 21st/22nd 16th Sussex (Yeo) Regt will carry out a raid on enemy's line about Q.8.c.8.8 with artillery co-operation.
2. OBJECT. To obtain prisoners and identifications and to harass the enemy.
3. STRENGTH. 1 Officer and 30 Other Ranks.
4. PROGRAMME.

Zero	Artillery bombardment of enemy's front line starts. Raiding party in position 100 yards from enemy's wire start crawling forward as far as possible.
Zero + 1 minute	Artillery lift over, leaving a box barrage. Party advance to a point fixed by reconnaissance just South of Q.8.c.8.8 and cut their way through enemy's wire.
Zero + 9 minutes	Party get through enemy's wire and work North up enemy's posts.
Zero + 12 minutes	Party return through enemy's wire.
Zero + 17 minutes	Artillery fire ceases.

5. MACHINE GUNS.
'B' Coy 74th M.G.Battn will co-operate with artillery by fire on flanks of portion of line attacked.
6. TRENCH MORTARS.
230th Light Trench Mortar Battery will create a diversion by firing bursts on road Q.14.a.6.2 to Q.14.a.7.8 and on road junction Q.14.d.4.9
7. SYNCHRONISATION OF WATCHES. An Officer from 16th Sussex, Right Group Artillery, 'B' Coy 74th M.G.Battn and 230th L.T.M.Battery will synchronise watches with a representative of Brigade Headquarters at Left Battalion Headquarters P.17.b.20.75 at 6.30 p.m.
8. ZERO HOUR will be notified later.
9. ACKNOWLEDGE.

C. Chaffer
Captain,
a/Brigade Major,
230th Infantry Brigade.

Issued at

Copy No, 1 File
2 16th Sussex
3 Right Group Artillery
4 'B' Coy 74th M.G.Bn.
5 230th L.T.M.Battery
6 74th Division
7 15th Suffolks)
8 231st Inf.Bde) for information
9)
10) War Diary.

Vol. 5

Headquarters,
230th Inf. Bde
(74th Division)

August 1918.

VOLUME No.

BRITISH SALONIKA FORCE

WAR DIARY.

VOL. No.	UNIT	PERIOD FROM	PERIOD TO
18.	Graves Reg. Unit Salonika	1. 7. 19	31. 7. 19
9	" " " Gallipoli	—	—
4. & 5	G. R. U. Aegean Islands	1. 6. 19 / 1. 7. 19	30. 6. 19 / 31. 7. 19
5.	G. R. U. Constantinople	1. 7. 19	31. 7. 19

A.P. & S.D., Ska. 774/1870/1 2000 11/7/18 Pap.

A Q

July 1916

6 Division

R/1/G

HEADQUARTERS
8 SEP. 1918

Headquarters
74th (Yeo) Division

Herewith War Diary of HQ 230th Inf Bde for the month of August last.

War Diaries of units of the Brigade for the same period will be forwarded very shortly.

[signature]
Brigadier General
Cmdg 230th Infantry Bde.

9/9/18

Army Form C. 2118.

REF MAP 36ᴬ S.E. 1:20000
230 Inf. Bde

HQ 230 Infy Bde
Aug. 1918.
Vol 5

Instructions regarding War Diaries and Intelligence Summaries are contained in F. S. Regs., Part II. and the Staff Manual respectively. Title pages will be prepared in manuscript.

B.E.F.

WAR DIARY
or
~~INTELLIGENCE SUMMARY.~~
(~~Erase heading not required.~~)

Place	Date	Hour	Summary of Events and Information	Remarks and references to Appendices
HAMEN ARTOIS	Aug. 1.		Weather fine.	
		10.30.	B.G.C. and Bn Commanders attended lecture and demonstration by Lt Genl MAXSE on Training, returned 5 p.m.	MAP 36ᴬ S.E. 1:20.000
			Orders received for this Brigade to relieve 231 Inf Bde in St VENANT Sector of front line on 4/5th Aug.	
			Arrangements made with 231 B. H.Q. about advance parties.	
	2	AM.	Rain wiped off all day – AM. Watched training of 15 Buffs.	
	3.		Showery.	
		AM	B.G.C. and B.M. motored to 231 Inf Bde and went round trenches ~~to~~ with a view to taking over.	
			G.S.O. III of 5th Army called.	
			Military medals granted to Pte SANDFORD & Pte NOAKES 16 Sussex for raid carried out in last tour.	
	4.		B.M. + B.I.O. went over to 231 Inf Bde for the relief.	
		9 pm	Relief began.	
	5.	1.30 am	Relief complete – ~~10 Buffs in right front~~ 10 Buffs right ~~left~~ front. 16 Sussex in ~~support~~ left front. 15 Buffs in support ~~at~~	
			The line extended from Q 8 a 32 to Canal at J 36 b 1.5	
			Day showery.	
		9 am	B.G.C. arrived at B.H.Q. P.7.C & assumed command of the sector	
		3 pm	Received information from the Division that part of the enemy line	

[signature]
B.M.
230 Inf Bde.

D. D. & L., London, E.C.
(A8004) Wt. W1771/M2031 750,000 5/17 Sch. 52 Forms/C2.118/14

2.

230 INF BDE
BEF

Instructions regarding War Diaries and Intelligence Summaries are contained in F. S. Regs., Part II. and the Staff Manual respectively. Title pages will be prepared in manuscript.

WAR DIARY
~~or~~
~~INTELLIGENCE SUMMARY.~~
~~(Erase heading not required.)~~

AUG 1918

Army Form C. 2118.

Place	Date	Hour	Summary of Events and Information	Remarks and references to Appendices
P.7.C.	5.		found evacuated opposite PACAUT WOOD opposite 4th Div on our right. Ordered patrolling to be very active — Patrols report enemy still holding trenches.	MAP 36ª SE 1:20,000.
		3.30pm	BGC went to Div H.Qrs to interview Corps Cmdr.	
	6.		Showery. A patrol of 10 Buffs returning from patrol was shot at by our men, Corpl. Killed and two men wounded.	
		11AM.	BGC held conference with Cos. OCRA, M.G.Bn and OC D Coy M.G. Bn at farm at P.14.d central. discussed proposed operation, also spoke on the Corps policy in case of enemy retirement.	
			During the afternoon and evening the enemy began to evacuate their trenches in front of 229 Inf. Bde on our right, & by midnight the 229th Inf had occupied the entire German front line except the left two or three posts.	
			Information received from prisoners that the entire German line in this part means to fall back for a distance of 2000 to 5000 metres.	
	7.		Buffs and Sussex both patrolled actively but were unable to advance their line as enemy still holding front line and their M.Gs were very active.	
			10th Buffs established new post at Q.8.a.5.2 in advance of our right flank.	

D. D. & L., London, E.C.
(A8001) Wt. W1771/M2031 750,000 5/17 Sch. 52 Forms/C2118/14

3

230 Inf Bde

BEF

Aug. 1918

Instructions regarding War Diaries and Intelligence Summaries are contained in F. S. Regs., Part II. and the Staff Manual respectively. Title pages will be prepared in manuscript.

WAR DIARY
or
INTELLIGENCE SUMMARY.
(Erase heading not required.)

Army Form C. 2118.

Place	Date	Hour	Summary of Events and Information	Remarks and references to Appendices
			Contd.	
Pyc	7.		B.G.C. went up to the front line of the Buffs and gave verbal instructions to O.C. 10 Buffs to push on at once. But O.C. Buffs asked if he might do it after dark.	MAP 36A SE 1/20000
		2pm	Received wire giving 229 Inf Bde line advanced about 1500x & instructions contained in wire to this Brigade to sweep up enemy line in a northerly direction	
		4pm	Enemy again reported holding trenches in front of us.	
		8.30pm	Patrols from 10 Buffs got into enemy trenches and found them unoccupied, worked up northwards to Rly at Q2a1.9. and got posts out onto road immediately East of enemy trenches - Touch obtained with 229 Inf Bde. Sussex told to push on.	
		6pm	2 Coys 15 Suffolks ordered to Amusoire - Haverskerque line to relieve one Coy each of Buffs and Sussex	
		11pm	Remaining two Coys Suffolks ordered to the A-H line and [illegible] to Home Farm P5d to be complete by 9am.	
		11.59pm	Sussex patrols over Lys and in Cornet Malo - Some enemy still in K32c western.	
	8	5am	16 Sussex along line Q2a11 to Q1b9.10. to K31d10.2 to K31b81 10 Buffs as before.	
		7am	B.G.C. issued orders for Bde to advance to objective line Q3d cent - Old Lys in Q3b & K33d to Canal at K33b22.	

[illegible] Major B.M. 230 Inf Bde

4

230 INF BDE

B.E.F.

Instructions regarding War Diaries and Intelligence Summaries are contained in F. S. Regs., Part II. and the Staff Manual respectively. Title pages will be prepared in manuscript.

WAR DIARY
or
INTELLIGENCE SUMMARY.
(*Erase heading not required.*)

AUG 1918

Army Form C. 2118.

Place	Date	Hour	Summary of Events and Information	Remarks and references to Appendices
PC 7 Q	8		4 MGs and 2 LTM's attached each attacking Battn.	MAP 36A SE 1:20,000
		1am	10 Buffs reached road from Q3d35 to Q3a83. 16 Sussex line of Old Lys Q3b27 to K33b12. Reported river 20 feet wide – All bridges destroyed except one at K33b11 which is swept by M.G. fire.– No enemy encountered during this advance but continuous M.G. & rifle fire.– A counter attack by about 100 enemy on right flank of the Buffs who at the moment were not in touch with the 229 Inf Bde. Several of the Enemy were killed by our L.G. fire but all the same our line was forced back a little to the line Q9a89 up to LA HENNERIE. The line shortly after advanced again after Houses Q3d and LE PACAUT had been bombarded and the objective was reached	
		8pm	finally along the Old RIVER LYS by 8pm and touch obtained with the next Bde on the right at post at Q4c cent with little Opposition–	
			During the night nothing of interest occurred and three bridges were put across the LYS in Q33d and bridge heads established on the East side.	
	9	330am	Received wire from Division saying that it is indicated that Enemy will probably continue to hold the line PARADIS (Q18c) Q4d cent K34c00 Canal at K34a02. K22d24 during the 9th and possibly the 10th Aug.	

[illegible] B.M.
230 Inf Bde

D. D. & L., London, E.C.
(A8004) Wt. W1771/M2031 750,000 5/17 Sch. 52 Forms/C2118/14

5

230 INF BDE

B.E.F

WAR DIARY
or
INTELLIGENCE SUMMARY.

(*Erase heading not required.*)

AUG 1918

Army Form C. 2118.

Instructions regarding War Diaries and Intelligence Summaries are contained in F. S. Regs., Part II. and the Staff Manual respectively. Title pages will be prepared in manuscript.

Place	Date	Hour	Summary of Events and Information	Remarks and references to Appendices
P.7.C	9.		Brigades instructed to endeavour by employing small forces to test strength of opposition in this line. If enemy shows any sign of withdrawal or weakness troops concerned will press forward at that point and exploit any success. This was repeated to all units concerned	MAP. 36^A S.E. 1:20.000
	~~10~~	10am.	The casualties that occurred during this advance consisted of 1 officer 16 Sussex ~~killed~~ wounded 1 officer 10 Buffs wounded - 40 OR killed and 14 wounded)	
LA HAYE		10am.	B.G.C went up the line & BHQ moved to LA HAYE Fm P.11.a	
		12.55pm	16 Sussex ~~report~~ patrol reports enemy with M.G holding post immediately in front of them also two other M.G.s which bother them.	
			10 Buffs patrol unable to get across the old Lys owing to our not having been able to put up bridges.	
			During evening M.Gs turned on to all known M.Gs	
		6.10pm	Received warning order from Division that 230 Inf Bde will take over the sector at present held by 229 Inf Bde in addition to that already held.	
		6.20pm	16 Sussex report that 2nd Lt WAUGH and a Corporal, after bombing an enemy M.G post rushed it and captured two prisoners - one of which gave very valuable information including the fact that the present line is held by the enemy in some strength but that they intend to retire on to the LESTREM LINE in 3 or 4 days.	

J. Duxton Major
BM 230 Inf Bde

D. D. & L., London, E.C.
(A8004) Wt. W1771/M2031 750,000 5/17 Sch. 52 Forms/C2118/14

6 · 230 INF BDE

Instructions regarding War Diaries and Intelligence Summaries are contained in F. S. Regs., Part II. and the Staff Manual respectively. Title pages will be prepared in manuscript.

B.E.F.

WAR DIARY
or
INTELLIGENCE SUMMARY.
(Erase heading not required.)

AUG. 1918

Army Form C. 2118.

Place	Date	Hour	Summary of Events and Information	Remarks and references to Appendices
P.11.a	9.	8pm	1 Coy of 15 Suffolks moved up from AMUSOIRE - HAVERSKERQUE line to Reserve line.	MAP 36A SE 1:20000
LA HAYE Fm.		11pm	Artillery and MGs turned on to all back areas and enemy works. No patrols other than defensive patrols sent out.	
	10		Quiet night - weather fine.	
		8am	Lt Col F. JARVIS 15 Suffks called on 229 Inf Bde and arranged the taking over from that Bde, of the sector on our right held by them.	
		9am	Issued orders for taking over the whole Divisional line which will now be disposed in depth. One Brigade holding front line with two Bns, and one in Support. One Brigade in support in Reserve and AMUSOIRE lines and one Brigade in Reserve at LA PIERRIERE, MICQUELLERIE & HAMET BILLET. Brigade disposed as follows 15 Suffolks to take over that held by 229th Bde 10 Buffs to take over that held by 16 Sussex in addition to what they already hold. 16 Sussex to form the Support in our old front and ~~Reserve~~ Support lines. Each front line Bn to hold line with two Coys, with one Coy in hidden position for counter attack and one company in a redoubt.	
		9.30am	BGRA & OC 117 Bde RFA called. 10.30 Am. GSO I called.	
		11Am.	BM went over to see 229 BDE to arrange relief.	

[signature] Major
BM 230 Inf Bde

D. D. & L., London, E.C.
(A8004) Wt. W1771/M2031 750,000 5/17 Sch. 52 Forms/C2118/14

7.

230 INF BDE

Instructions regarding War Diaries and Intelligence Summaries are contained in F. S. Regs., Part II. and the Staff Manual respectively. Title pages will be prepared in manuscript.

B.E.F

WAR DIARY
or
INTELLIGENCE SUMMARY.
(Erase heading not required.)

Aug. 1918

Army Form C. 2118.

Place	Date	Hour	Summary of Events and Information	Remarks and references to Appendices
LAHAYE FARM	10.		Some enemy shelling during the day especially on CARVIN RD in right Bde Sector and on CALONNE Area in our Sector. During the early part of the night Artillery and M.G.s fired heavily on enemy's back areas	MAP. 36a SE 1:20,000
	11.		Relief complete by 1.30 am. Quiet night except some artillery fire in vicinity of BERKSHIRE Fm probably meant for some 60 pdrs there on each side of the road. Patrols during the night and early morning met everywhere by enemy M.G fire, one man 10 Buffs missing believed killed. B.G.C. visited the right of the line & saw O.C. 15th Suffolks. During the morning G.O.C. GSO I and AA & QMG called. G.O.C. stated that he had indications that enemy intended to retire from Old Brit Lys and wanted active patrolling. Heavy shelling during the night on vicinity of BERKSHIRE Fm and also in St FLORIS.	
	12.		Heavy artillery fire at 3 am in vicinity of WINDY CORNER. From patrol reports of 10 Buffs it is suspected that enemy has retired further back beyond the old Lys line. B.G.C. went up to see O.C. 10 Buffs & placed Capt C.P. Ponsonby in command of Buffs vice Capt FRIEND (who was acting vice Lt Col BISLETON on leave) because Capt. FRIEND has ordered no forward move without orders.	

J Burton Major
BM. 230 Inf Bde

D. D. & L., London, E.C.
(A8001) Wt. W1771/M2031 750,000 5/17 Sch. 52 Forms/C2118/14

8

230 Inf Bde

BEF

Instructions regarding War Diaries and Intelligence Summaries are contained in F. S. Regs., Part II. and the Staff Manual respectively. Title pages will be prepared in manuscript.

WAR DIARY
~~or~~
~~INTELLIGENCE SUMMARY.~~
(~~Erase heading not required.~~)

Aug 1918

Army Form C. 2118.

Place	Date	Hour	Summary of Events and Information	Remarks and references to Appendices
LA HAYE FM	12	9.30 pm	A minor operation by which 10th Buffs were to advance their line, was planned as follows:- At Zero 9.30 pm an artillery barrage was put down between the Lys Canal and the Old River Lys about 500x behind enemy's front line - this crept back onto his front line and then advanced again followed by the infantry patrols backed by platoons, intending to seize and hold the enemy's front line - Considerable opposition was met especially from M.Gs on the front & flanks - The patrols were nowhere able to get beyond the enemy's wire. The enemy then delivered a counter attack ~~from~~ between the Lys and the Old River Lys, this was partially met by part of a platoon with an L.G. which scattered the enemy attacking them causing casualties.	MAP 36a SE 1:20,000
			As the line of enemy's wire was so close to our front line, the order was given to retire onto our old position and not consolidate where they were-	
			The casualties of the Buffs amounted to 3 O.R. killed 15 wounded and 8 missing.	

[signature] Major
Bm 230 Inf Bde

9 · 230 Inf Bde

WAR DIARY
or
~~INTELLIGENCE SUMMARY.~~
(~~Erase heading not required.~~)

Aug 1918

B.E.F

Army Form C. 2118.

Instructions regarding War Diaries and Intelligence Summaries are contained in F. S. Regs., Part II. and the Staff Manual respectively. Title pages will be prepared in manuscript.

Place	Date	Hour	Summary of Events and Information	Remarks and references to Appendices
LA HAYE FM.	12.	10 pm.	The whole operation was much hampered by (1) the night being extremely dark, (2) by there being enough enemy gas shelling to make it necessary to put on S.B.Rs (3) by our barrage being so thin as to be practically useless.	MAP 36a SE 1:20,000
	13.		Fine day. During the morning the Eastern end of St FLORIS was fairly heavily shelled with 8" and 5.9"s	
		2 pm.	G.S.O. I called also G.S.O. II of Corps.	
			Orders issued for the relief of 10 Buffs by 16 Sussex on night of 14/15 in left Bn Subsection.	
	15.		Fine day. Relief complete 1.5 am	
		9.30 am	B.M. went over to 229 Inf Bde to arrange their command relief i.e. 230 Bde to be relieved in line by 231st Bde and to relieve 229th Bde in support.	
	16	4.30 am.	During the early morning, there was some gas shelling round B.H.Q. making it necessary to put on S.B.Rs.	
	~~16~~		Weather fine. B.G.C. 231 Inf Bde called and went over the Bde Sector.	
		12.30.	Corps Commander called and saw B.G.C.	
			Letter received from Div saying G.O.C. approves of the disposition for defence of this sector with the exception that he wishes the line of resistance to become the line of resistance near the front line	
			[signature] Bm 230 Inf Bde.	

D. D. & L., London, E.C. (A8001) Wt. W1771/M2031 750,000 5/17 Sch. 52 Forms/C2.118/14

10.

230 INF BDE

WAR DIARY
or
~~INTELLIGENCE SUMMARY.~~
(Erase heading not required.)

Army Form C. 2118.

Instructions regarding War Diaries and Intelligence Summaries are contained in F. S. Regs., Part II. and the Staff Manual respectively. Title pages will be prepared in manuscript.

BEF

Aug 1918

Place	Date	Hour	Summary of Events and Information	Remarks and references to Appendices
LA HAYE	17.	12.30am	Relief complete – Bde went into support.	
		9.30am	BGC 231 arrived and assumed command –	MAP
BUSNE			Weather dull & threatening with wind	36A SE.
CHATEAU		10am	BGC met G.O.C. at BUSNE CHATEAU.	1:20,000
			BHQ moved to BUSNE CHATEAU, units disposed as follows	
			15 Buffs 2 Coys in Reserve line & 2 Coys in AMUSOIRES – HAVERSKERQUE line	
			10 Buffs — do — — do —	
			The boundary between the two the old inter Bde boundary.	
			16 Sussex HAMET BILLET	
			LTMB — do —	
			Wiring on Reserve line to be continued by the Garrison	
			Arrangements made for as much harvesting as possible by Garrison of A.O.H. line & by Reserve Bn at HAMET BILLET.	
		3.30pm	Capt J.F.A. LEWIS PEMBROKE YEO reported as "learner" for attachment	
	18.		Heavy showers in early morning but cleared up by midday –	
			BGC with G.O.C. visited Div Reception Camp at LINGHEM –	
	19.		Fine day work on Reserve line and Harvesting progressing well.	
		3.30pm	BGC met all Combatant Officers near TIBBS FARM and discussed last tour in the trenches.	
	20	10am	G.O.C. GSO I AA & QMG called.	

Meister Major
BM. 230 Inf Bde

D. D. & L., London, E.C.
(A8001) Wt. W1771/M2031 750,000 5/17 Sch. 52 Forms/C2118/14

Instructions regarding War Diaries and Intelligence Summaries are contained in F. S. Regs., Part II. and the Staff Manual respectively. Title pages will be prepared in manuscript.

WAR DIARY
or
INTELLIGENCE SUMMARY.
(Erase heading not required.)

Army Form C. 2118.

Place	Date	Hour	Summary of Events and Information	Remarks and references to Appendices
BUSNE CHATEAU	20		B.G.C. started on a weeks leave to HOULGATE near Havre. Lt Col JARVIS took command of the Bde.	MAP 36A SE 1:20000
	21.		Weather fine and hot. Orders received for Divisional sector to be extended to the right to include one more Battn sector. Each half of whole sector to be held in future by 6 platoons as Strong Point garrison, remainder of two Bns at present in Reserve and A-H line to be billetted in ROBECQ & ST FLORIS.	
LA HAYE	22	3pm	B.H.Q. closed at BUSNE CHATEAU which will in future be occupied by D.H.Q. & opened at LA HAYE Fm. Received warning order that 229 Inf Bde will relieve 231 in front line on night 24/25th Aug. Latter to go into support. The 230 Bde into Reserve.	
	23	12 N.	Corps Comdr called – Weather extremely hot.	
	24.		Slight showers in early morning.	
	25.		Relief of 230 I Bde in line of Retention by 231 Inf Bde complete by 2.40 am	
		10am	Command passed to B.G.C. 230 Inf Bde. at LA HAYE Fm. B.H.Q. opened at P.7.C.	
		5pm	Orders received for Bde to proceed ST HILAIRE area tomorrow changing places with 176 Bde.	
		8pm	Started training. Lt Col Jarvis dined with Corps HQ.	

[illegible] Major
B.M. 230 Inf Bde

B. 230 Inf Bde BEF

WAR DIARY
or
INTELLIGENCE SUMMARY.
(*Erase heading not required.*)

Aug 1918

Army Form C. 2118.

Instructions regarding War Diaries and Intelligence Summaries are contained in F. S. Regs., Part II. and the Staff Manual respectively. Title pages will be prepared in manuscript.

Place	Date	Hour	Summary of Events and Information	Remarks and references to Appendices
P.y.C.	26		Rained all night -	MAP 36A SE 1/20,000
		10 am	BGC 176 Inf Bde called -	
ST HILAIRE		3 pm	176 Inf Bde marched to BUIRE and 230 Inf Bde marched to ST HILAIRE area and arrived in billets 6.30 pm. Units as follows BHQ & LTMB ST HILAIRE 10 Buffs 15 Suffolks at ST HILAIRE, LESPESSES and COTTES. 16 Sussex BOURECQ	
	27	11.30 am	Army Comdr called with GOC to say good bye.	
		6 pm	Orders received to move on night 28/29 by train to HEILLY STATION.	
	28.		Wet day. BGC arrived back from leave.	
		10.40 pm	BHQ entrained for HEILLY. Remainder of Bde entrained at intervals up till 4 pm on 29th.	
	29.	1.30 pm	BHQ arrived HEILLY - weather fine - marched to BEHENCOURT on arrival	
BAISIEUX			all billets changed. BHQ to BAISIEUX. Bns to remain bivouacked at HEILLY. Bde ready to move at short notice. Now in III Corps IV Army.	
	30.	10.30 am	Bde [illegible] [illegible] - Warning received that Div will take over from 58 Div	
	31	2.40 pm	Received orders for units to embus at HEILLY - Transport to proceed by road to MARICOURT - Guides to meet busses at MARICOURT -	
		6 pm	Busses started arrived [illegible] [illegible] 8.[illegible] when handed busses over to 173 Inf Bde. No guides at MARICOURT but [illegible] HQ then informed us they were at X cross Rds 3 miles E of MARICOURT where we found them. Road [illegible] congested. Bns found guides about 3.30/4 am and bivouacked at [illegible] 4.30 am	
			[illegible]	[illegible] Major Bm 230 Inf Bde

D. D. & L., London, E.C.
(A8001) Wt. W1771/M2031 750,000 5/17 Sch. 52 Forms/C2118/14

13r 230 INF BDE

Instructions regarding War Diaries and Intelligence Summaries are contained in F. S. Regs., Part II. and the Staff Manual respectively. Title pages will be prepared in manuscript.

BEF

WAR DIARY
or
INTELLIGENCE SUMMARY.
(Erase heading not required.)

Aug 1918

Army Form C. 2118.

Place	Date	Hour	Summary of Events and Information	Remarks and references to Appendices
MAP 62c 1/40000 F23. cent.			Effective Strength of units 10th Buffs 26 Offrs 766 OR 15th Suffolks 28 " 781 " 16 Sx. 28 " 786 " LTMB 4 " 41 " During the month the health of the troops has been good. 31. Aug. 1918	MAP 36 NE. 1:20000

[illegible] Major
BdeMajor
230 Inf Bde

D. D. & L., London, E.C. (A8004) Wt. W1771/M2031 750,000 5/17 Sch. 52 Forms/C2118/14

SECRET Copy No. 2.....

230th Infantry Brigade Order No.47.

Ref.Map:- 36A.1:40,000. 1-8-18.

1. The 230th Infantry Brigade will relieve 231st Infantry Brigade in the ST. FLORIS Sector on the night 4th/5th August.

2. Relief will be carried out as per Table attached.

3. All documents and maps relating to Divisional Reserve area will be handed over and receipts taken and those referring to ST. FLORIS Section, together with photographs and trench stores, will be taken over from opposite numbers. and receipts given

4. Details of relief not dealt with in these orders will be arranged direct between commanding officers concerned.

5. Advanced parties consisting of :-
   C.Os. & Adjutants (if C.Os. have not already seen over this section of the line).

   Front Line Company commanders:-
   1 Officer per Coy. for Coys other than Front Line Coys.
   Battalion Intelligence Officer.
   " Lewis Gun Officer.
   " Signal Officor.

   will march up on Friday 2nd August and will come out again to their Battalions on night Saturday 3rd/4th.

6. Command of the ST. FLORIS Section will pass to B.G.C., 230th Infantry Brigade at 9-30 a.m. on 5th August.

7. Bde.H.Q., will close at HAM EN ARTOIS at 9-30 a.m. on 5th inst. and open at P.7.c.1.5. at the same hour.

8. Completion of relief will be immediately wired to 231st Infantry Brigade at P.7.c.1.5. using the code word SPOT.

9. All Guards on Bde. H.Q on road and Canal Bridges will be relieved by 6.p.m.

10. ACKNOWLEDGE.

J Thruston

Major,
Brigade Major.
230th Infantry Brigade.

Issued at :

Copies to No.1. 74th Division.
2. File.
3. 229th Inf.Bde.
4. 231st Inf.Bde.
5. Buffs.
6. Suffolks.
7. Sussex.
8. L.T.M.B.
No.9. Bde.Signals Officer.
10. 74th M.G.Battalion.
11. R.M.R.E.
12. Field Ambulance.
13. Staff Captain.
14. War Diary.
15. " "
16. " "

RELIEF TABLE.

issued with 230th Infantry Brigade Order No.47 dated 1-8-18.

Serial No.	UNIT.	From	To relieve	Location	Remarks.
1.	10th Buffs.	LA MIQUELLERIE.	10th K.S.L.I.	Right Subsection H.Q.,P.11.a.9.2.	Not to cross AIRE - LA BASSEE Canal before 9 p.m.
2.	16th Sussex.	GUARBECQUE.	25th R.W.F	Left Subsection. H.Q.,P.5.a.2.0.	- do -
3.	15th Suffolks.	HAM-EN-ARTOIS.	24th W.R.	Bde. Reserve. H.Q.,HAMET BILLET.	Relief to be complete by 7 p.m. ~~Not to reach HAMET BILLET before 9-30 p.m.~~
4.	230th L.T.M.B.	- do -	231st L.T.M.B.	H.Q. P.1.d.4.1 4 Guns in Line.	Relief to be complete by 8 p.m.

NOTE. Usual distances will be preserved between Companies.

S E C R E T.   Copy No......7

ADMINISTRATIVE ORDERS

relative to

230th Infantry Brigade Order No.47 of 1-8-18.

TRENCH STORES, AMMUNITION, GRENADES, etc.

A List of Trench Stores and S.A.A. taken over will be forwarded to Bde.H.Q.,by 9 a.m. 6th inst, on the attached pro forma.

BAGGAGE WAGONS.

Baggage Wagons will report to Units' Transport Lines at 9 a.m. August 4th for conveyance of kits to new area and will rejoin 449 Coy. A.S.C. the same day.

"B" TEAMS.

A Motor Lorry will report to each Unit at 9-30 a.m. 4th inst, to convey blankets etc., of "B" Teams to the Divisional Reception Camp LINGHEM. On arrival at LINGHEM Lorries will be handed over to O.C.,"B" Teams 231st Infantry Brigade.

SUPPLIES.

On and after 5th inst Supplies will be drawn at MAZINGHEM at 6-30 a.m.

INDENTS.

Indents for R.E. Material and S.A.A.,Grenades, etc., must reach Bde.H.Q. by 1st D.R.L.S. each day.

ACKNOWLEDGE.

Percy W. Rockville
Capt,
Staff Capt.
230th Infantry Brigade.

2-8-18.

Issued at

Copies to :- No.1. O.C.Buffs.
2. Suffolks.
3. Sussex.
4. L.T.M.B.
5. 449 Coy. A.S.C.
No.6. Bde.Supply Officer.
7. Brigade Major.
8. Staff Capt.
9. File.

L I S T of P A P E R S in RESERVE BRIGADE FILE handed over to 231st Infantry Brigade by 230th Infantry Brigade on 5th August 1918.

---

1. DEFENCE SCHEME.
2. SUPPLEMENTARY INSTRUCTIONS for Brigade in Reserve.
3. REPORT and RECONNAISSANCE of Tracks Eastwards (by 229th Inf.Bde).
4. " " " " " South-Eastwards.
5. " " " " " North-Eastwards.
6. TACTICAL EXERCISE WITHOUT TROOPS for practice in move Eastwards.
7. Copy of letter to 74th Division on points noticed when carrying out 6.
8. Copy reply from Division.

---

9. Positions of A.A. Lewis Guns in Reserve Brigade area.
10. Notes on training facilities with copy wire re Ranges.

<u>Handed over by</u>:-

[illegible] Major
B.M. 230 Inf Bde
5/8/18

<u>Taken over by</u>:-

H.P. Wood Lt
for B.M.
231. Inf Bde.

S E C R E T. Copy No. 10...

230th Infantry Brigade Order No.48.

Ref.Map:- 36A. S.E. & N.E. 1:20,000. 6-8-18.

1. The inter-battalion boundary in the ST FLORIS Section will in future be as follows:-
   K.32.c.0.2. - Q.1.b.1.9. - Q.1.a.central - P.12.b.3.8. - thence as at present.

2. The necessary amendment is to be made in all Defence Schemes.

3. The Os.C. 10th Buffs and 16th Sussex will arrange mutually for the taking over and handing over respectively of the portions of the support and front lines involved, during the night of the 7th/8th.

4. The O.C. 15th Suffolks will detail one Company to take over those portions of the front and support lines at present held by the 10th Buffs between the right of the Brigade boundary and the railway in Q.1.b.c and d, during the night of the 9th /10th. Details of this relief to be arranged between the Commanders of Battalions concerned.

5. The troops of the 10th Buffs so relieved should preferably be accommodated in the reserve line, and in the HAVERSKERQUE - AMUSOIRES line also, if insufficient accommodation exists in the former.

6. ACKNOWLEDGE.

Major,
Brigade Major.
230th Infantry Brigade.

Issued at

Copies to No.1.	O.C.Buffs.	No.6.	74th Division.
2.	Suffolks.	7.	Defence Scheme.
3.	Sussex.	8.	C.R.A.
4.	L.T.M.B.	9.	229th Inf.Bde.
5.	M.G.Battalion	10.	File.

S E C R E T. Copy No.7...

230th Infantry Brigade Order No.42.

Ref.Map:- 36A. S.E. & N.E. 1:20,000. 6-8-18.

1. The inter-battalion boundary in the ST FLORIS Section will in future be as follows:-
K.32.c.0.2. - Q.1.b.1.9. - Q.1.a.central - P.12.b.8.8. - thence as at present.

2. The necessary amendment is to be made in all Defence Schemes.

3. The Os.C. 10th Buffs and 16th Sussex will arrange mutually for the taking over and handing over respectively of the portions of the support and front lines involved, during the night of the 7th/8th.

4. The O.C. 15th Suffolks will detail one Company to take over those portions of the front and support lines at present held by the 10th Buffs between the right of the Brigade boundary and the railway in Q.1.b.c and d, during the night of the 9th /10th. Details of this relief to be arranged between the Commanders of Battalions concerned.

5. The troops of the 10th Buffs so relieved should preferably be accommodated in the reserve line, and in the HAVERSKERQUE - AMUSOIRES line also, if insufficient accommodation exists in the former.

6. ACKNOWLEDGE.

Major,
Brigade Major.
230th Infantry Brigade.

Issued at

Copies to No.1. O.C.Buffs. No.6. 74th Division.
2. Suffolks. 7. Defence Scheme. ✓
3. Sussex. 8. C.R.A.
4. L.T.M.B. 9. 229th Inf.Bde.
5. M.G.Battalion. 10. File.

B112/9

S E C R E T.

In future, Brigade Operation Orders will be issued to the Brigade Group and Division as follows, and a list will not be given on each copy other than those extra to this list:-

No. 1	10 Buffs
2	15 Suffolks
3	16 Sussex
4	'B' Coy, M.G.Battn
5	231st Field Ambulance.
6	R.A.R.E.
7	449 Coy A.S.C.
8	230th L.T.M.B.
9	O.C. Forward Group, R.F.A.
10	B.G.C. 230th Inf.Bde.
11	Brigade Major
12	Staff Captain
13	Bde Transport Officer
14	Bde Signals Officer
15) 16) 17)	War Diary
18	File
19	74th Division

G Ruxton

Major,
Brigade Major,
230th Infantry Bde.

10th August 1918.

SECRET. Copy No. 2....

230th INFANTRY BRIGADE ORDER. No.50.

Reference Map 36A. 10-8-18.

1. The enemy's position along the right bank of the BOURRE River and thence Southwards to the NEUVILLE-PARADIS Road appears to be well organised and held in some strength, probably with the object of covering the completion of a more permanent line which has been located by aeroplane photographs and extends from the West side of NEUF BERQUIN through L.13, 19, 25 to 31 and thence West of LESTREM and the LAWE.

2. Our further progress Eastwards depends upon the progress made by the two flank Divisions. The present front line will be organised as a strong outpost position. Patrolling will be very active and every endeavour will be made to discover any weakening of the enemy's defence.

3. The Division is being organised in depth with this Brigade as advanced guard Brigade and the 229th Brigade holding the Reserve Line, which remains the main line of Retention.

4. In accordance with above policy the Brigade will on the night of the 10th/11th be disposed as follows :-

Right Front Battalion.	Suffolks holding from Q.17.a.1.8. to Q.3.d.9.7.
Left Front Battalion.	Buffs holding from Q.3.d.9.7. to Canal K.33.b.4.1.
Support Battalion.	Sussex in the old front and support lines - 2 Companies in rear of each front Battalion.

5. Dividing line between front Battalions from West to East will be Q.7.d.central - road junction Q.9.a.7.9. - cross roads in Q.3.d.4.4. - thence along North bank of CLARENCE to Q.4.b.2.0. (all inclusive to right Battalion) thence due Eastwards through Q.5. and Q.6.

6. During the night of the 10/11th the Buffs will take over that portion of their new front held by the Sussex and the Suffolks will take over the front now held by the 229th Brigade. Details of these reliefs will be arranged between the C.O's of the Buffs and Sussex and between the C.O., Suffolks and Staff of 229th Brigade.

7. The Sussex on relief will be disposed as in para 4, Battalion H.Q. retaining its present position.

8. The Suffolks and Buffs will both be disposed at the earliest opportunity as follows :-
   (a) Two Companies holding a line of observation and a line of resistance.
   (b) One Company detailed for immediate counter-attack in case line of resistance is pierced.
   (c) One Company with the Battalion Command Post in a redoubt organised for all round defence. These redoubts to be sited about 1200 yards from line of observation.

9. Pending construction of command posts, the O.C. Suffolks will establish his H.Q. not further West than the Western edge of Q.14. and O.C.Buffs not further West than K.31.c.central.

10. O.C. D.Coy, 74th M.G.Battalion will arrange in conjunction with the two front Battalion Commanders to distribute his machine guns 4 forward and 4 rear in each Battalion Sub-section. The forward guns adjacent to or in the ~~support~~ line of resistance line and rear guns in the redoubt line.

11. Completion of relief will be wired to Bde.H.Q. using the following Code Words :-

Buffs.	CLARET.
Suffolks.	SHERRY.
Sussex.	PORT.
M.G.Coy.	BRANDY.

12. No change will be made for the present in the disposition of the 230th L.T.M.B.

13. Command of the present 229th Brigade Section will pass to 230th Brigade on completion of relief by Suffolks.

14. Brigade report centre will remain for the present at P.11.a.8.2.

15. ACKNOWLEDGE.

J Johnston
Major,
Brigade Major.
230th Infantry Brigade.

Issued at 9 am

Copies to No.1. 74th Division.
2. File.
3. War Diary.
4. " "
5. " "
6. Buffs.
7. Suffolks.
8. Sussex.
9. L.T.M.B.
10. B.Coy.M.G.Bn.
11. 74th M.G.Battn.
No.12. R.A.R.E.
13. 231st Fd.Ambce.
14. 449 Coy.A.S.C.
15. 229th Inf.Bde.
16. 182nd Inf.Bde.
17. 11th Inf.Bde.
18. 117th Bde.R.F.A.
19. B.T.O.
20. B.G.C.,230th Inf.Bde.
21. Brigade Major.
22. Staff Captain.

S E C R E T. Copy No. 6...

230th INFANTRY BRIGADE ORDER No. 51.

11th August 1918

1. The Advance Brigade is required to slowly advance its line with the double object of helping the forward movement of the Division on the right and of maintaining the closest possible touch with the enemy so as to discover any signs of his withdrawal.

2. It is considered that this may best be effected by carrying out small local operations of a surprise nature, especially in the area South of the OLD LIN - one or two Field Guns being specially brought forward for any particular enterprise.

3. As a preliminary to this proposal it is essential to determine by reconnaissance the nature and proximity of the enemy's defences opposite our front. These reconnaissances must be carried out nightly and it will be conducive to the success of any enterprise subsequently undertaken, and arising out of those reconnaissances, if the reconnoitring parties are changed as much as possible, for in this way more men will have been enabled to acquire personal knowledge of the terrain to be traversed and of the enemy lines.

4. The Companies in the front line must necessarily be relieved frequently, but these reliefs must not interfere with the local operations described above.

5. Battalion Commanders in front line will draw up schemes for local operations in accordance with above and will communicate same to Brigade Headquarters as soon as possible.

6. ACKNOWLEDGE.

[signature] Major
Brigade Major
~~Brigadier-General~~,
~~Commanding~~ 230th Infantry Brigade.

Copies to:-
No. 1 Buffs
2 Suffolks
3 Sussex
4 O.C. Artillery Group.
5 Brigade Major
6 File.

SECRET.

230th BRIGADE ORDER No.52. 12-8-18.

1. In the event of it not having been found possible to advance our line East of the OLD LYS, K.33.d.central and Q.3.b.central before 8-30 p.m. to-day the following operation will be carried out at 9 p.m. :-

2. All the troops between the Canal in K.33.b. and the railway in Q.3.d. will be withdrawn to a general line 200 yards West of the OLD LYS, withdrawal to be completed by 9 p.m.

3. At 9 p.m. the artillery will put down a barrage between the Canal and the railway on a general North and South line through ENNIS K.34.c.7.8. This barrage will creep Westwards to about the road running due South from the FERRY, K.33.b.4.2. and then halt prior to moving back Eastwards to its starting line.

4. Patrols backed up by platoons are to be held ready to advance behind the barrage as soon as it has commenced to move Eastwards with the object of :-
(a) Capturing or killing the enemy post garrisons already located in to-day's reconnaissance.
(b) Endeavouring to establish themselves (and consolidate) in the enemy front system in K.34.c. (Western portion) and possibly also in the North West portion of Q.4.a.

5. Arrangements must be made to exploit any success thus gained by moving forward Companies to support advanced platoons which may have succeeded in establishing themselves in the enemy's front system.

6. It is expected that the barrage will last for about 7 minutes only from start to finish, but precise times will be communicated later by wire. All watches will be synchronised at 7 p.m.

Sgd. A.A.KENNEDY, Brig.Gen.
Commdg. 230th Inf.Bde.

5 p.m.

Copies to O.C. Buffs.
Suffolks.
C.R.A.

COPY WIRE.

FEDI.

B.M.168.   12th.

Reference para 3 of Brigade Order No.52 just issued AAA Barrage will now commence 9-30 p.m. and last for 10 minutes AAA Patrols can safely commence to move forward to OLD LYS at zero plus 5 at which hour barrage leaves FERRY road and comes down on enemy front line until zero plus 8 AAA At zero plus 8 barrage moves back to starting point ENNIS line until zero plus 10 when it finishes AAA Patrols should not be within 100 yards of enemy front line until zero plus 8 AAA Withdrawal West of OLD LYS should not be completed 9-30 p.m. AAA Acknowledge   Addressed FEDI repeated FEFI and FEQU

FEQI

6-15 p.m.

"A" Form.

Army Form C. 2121.
(In pads of 100.)

MESSAGES AND SIGNALS.

No. of Message............

Prefix.......... Code .... m. | Words. | Charge.

Office of Origin and Service Instructions.

Sent
At .... m.
To ....
By ....

This message is on a/c of:
.... *Service.*
(Signature of "Franking Officer.")

Recd. at ...... m.
Date ....
From ....
By ....

TO 23rd BDE

Sender's Number.	Day of Month.	In reply to Number.	AAA
* W 573	13		

In	view	of	enclosed
message	from	67 RC	I
have	ordered	D	Coy
to	withdraw	to	original
position	where	they	will
be	relieved	by	support
Coy	[illegible]	I	have
also	ordered	right	Coy
to	withdraw	and	these
will	be	relieved	by
counter	attack	coy	aaa
in	view	of	fact
that	suggested	conditions	would
only	[illegible]	for	in
front	of	present	position
[illegible]	do	not	consider
it	worth	while	doing

From 10 BUFFS
Place
Time 1.5 am

The above may be forwarded as now corrected.
(Z)
.... *Censor.*

Signature of Addresser or person authorised to telegraph in his name.

Capt
10th BUFFS

*This line, except A A A, should be erased if not required.

Wt. W 3253/P511. 500,000 Pads. 1/18. B. & S. Ltd. (E2389.)

Army Form C. 2123.
(In books of 100.)

"C" Form.
MESSAGES AND SIGNALS.

No. of Message ________

Prefix SM Code MD Words 66	Received.	Sent, or sent out.	Office Stamp.
£ s. d.	From FRC	At ________ m.	FEDI 12 8 18
Charges to Collect	By [illegible]	To ________	
Service Instructions FRC		By ________	

Handed in at FRC Office 1220 m. Received 1230 m.

TO FEDI

* Sender's Number	Day of Month.	In reply to Number	AAA
1	12		

OC D COY is withdrawing on to road 50 yards EAST of LYS RIVER as he is enfiladed from both flanks and has many casualties aaa Do you wish him to go back to his original POSITION west of LYS RIVER or dig in where he is he says impossible to take position without another and much more effective arty preparation aaa

FROM FRC
PLACE & TIME

* This line should be erased if not required.

8310—W.528—100,000—10/5/17—E.P.Co.—(E1213).

To/

B.M. 230th Inf. Bde. 13-8.18.

Herewith report of Right Sector Coy. Commander.

H.T.B. Barnard
Lieut
for Major.

REPORT BY CAPT. C.E. HATFEILD, O.C. 'A' Coy.

At Zero + 5' my company advanced towards its objective, but owing to the dark night and big intervals, touch was soon lost.

The right platoon reached its objective with little opposition except from a M.G. on its right flank.

The right centre platoon was last seen about 200 yds from its objective, since when nothing has been heard of it with the exception of two men who kept in touch with the right platoon.

The left centre platoon reached the enemy wire in front of its right flank without opposition, the remainder of the platoon got within 100 yds of the wire, when heavy enemy fire consisting of M.G.s Minenwerfers & rifles was opened on it.

The left platoon encountered heavy M.G. & rifle fire from the moment it started to advance. When within 150 yds. the enemy, numbering about 40, counter-attacked and forced the platoon back on to the OLD LYS RIVER.

The positions of these platoons were maintained under continuous fire until I received the order to withdraw to my original position.

The dividing line between the Left Centre & Right Centre platoons was the RAILWAY.

C.E. Hatfield Capt
OC A Coy
10th Buffs

13/8/18.

REPORT OF OPERATIONS 12/13 – 8 – 18.

With reference to the attempted advance this morning I beg to report as follows –

I had two platoons in the front line and 2 in support. At zero + 5 the leading platoons went forward preceded by patrols & crossed the right & left bridges in the left Company sector.

I went with the left support platoon. The right platoon came under intense MG fire after it had advanced 100x, & were never able to get any further.

The left platoon managed by making rushes to get on about 250 yards & were then held up by direct MG fire from the front and enfilade fire from their left rear across the Canal. They were also enfiladed from 2 MG's in Strong point K34C15 to which I have referred in my patrol reports.

When here I got in touch with the right platoon & they tried again to advance, without success, so I gave orders for both platoons to fall back & reorganize on the line of the Ferry Road & subsequently, on receipt of orders, withdrew them over the Canal.

It seemed to me that a much stronger barrage is necessary

to have any effect on the M.G.s in position there.

I cannot give full particulars of Casualties at the moment

F D Wilkinson Lt.
O C D Coy
10th The Buffs.

S E C R E T. Copy No. 18

230th INFANTRY BRIGADE ORDER No.53.

Reference Map:- 36a, 1:20,000. 13th August 1918

1. On the night of the 14/15th August the 16th Sussex will relieve the 10th Buffs in the Left Subsection of the Brigade Sector.

2. 16th Sussex will be disposed in the same manner as the 10th Buffs.

3. 10th Buffs will move completely to the position at present occupied by 16th Sussex.

4. Details of relief will be arranged between C.O's concerned. Completion of relief will be notified by wire by code words as follows:-

10th Buffs	"Satisfied"
16th Sussex	"Content"

5. ACKNOWLEDGE.

Major,
Brigade Major,
230th Infantry Brigade.

Copies issued as per this
Office BMZ/9 of 10/8/18.

Copy No.20 182 Inf.Bde.

S E C R E T. Copy No. 18

230th INFANTRY BRIGADE ORDER No.54

Ref.Map:- 36A.S.E. 1/20,000. 15-8-18.

1. The 230th Infantry Brigade will be relieved in the line by the 231st Infantry Brigade on the night August 16th/17th.

2. On relief the 230th Infantry Brigade will take over responsibility for the Reserve Line from 229th Infantry Brigade.

3. The 15th Suffolks and 10th Buffs will be responsible for manning the Reserve Line.
Two Coys of each Battalion will therefore man the Reserve Line and two Coys of each Battalion will occupy the AMUSOIRES - HAVERSKERQUE line.
The dividing line between the two Battalions will be the inter-battalion boundary line.

4. Relief will be carried out as per table on reverse.

5. C.Coy M.G.Battn. at present attached to 229th Bde will come under the orders of B.G.C.,230th Infantry Brigade.

6. The detachment Field Ambulance at present under orders of B.G.C., 230th Infantry Brigade will come under the orders of the A.D.M.S.

7. Defence Instructions, aeroplane and special maps will be handed over.

8. Details of relief will be arranged direct between Units concerned.

9. 1 Section 229th L.T.M.B. at present attached 230th Infantry Brigade will, on relief, rejoin 229th Infantry Brigade at HAM-EN-ARTOIS.
~~1 Section 230th Inf.Bde.L.T.M.B.will remain in the line and come under the orders of 231st Infantry Brigade.~~

10. Command of advanced Brigade will pass to B.G.C.,231st Infantry Brigade at ~~10~~ 9.30 a.m. on 17th inst.

11. Relief to be reported by following code words to present Bde.H.Q:-

10th Buffs.	GROUSE.
15th Suffolks.	PARTRIDGE.
16th Sussex.	PHEASANT.
L.T.M.B.	DUCK.

12. ACKNOWLEDGE.

J. Brunton
Major,
Brigade Major.
230th Infantry Brigade.

Issued at

Copies to :- Group as per B.M.Z/9 of 10-8-18.
Copy No. 20. 11th Infantry Brigade.
21. 182nd " "
22. 229th. " "
23. 231st " "
24. D.A.D.M.S. 74th Division.
25. 74th M.G.Battalion.

R E L I E F   T A B L E.

U N I T.	From	Relieved by	To.	At present occupied by
230th Bde.H.Q.	P.11.a.9.1.	231st Bde.H.Q.	LABIETTE FARM. P.27.b.1.2.	229th Bde.H.Q.
10th Buffs.	Old front & Support Lines.	10th K.S.L.I.	Old Reserve Line & AMUSOIRES - HAVERSKERQUE Line N. of inter-battalion boundary.	16th Devons.
15th Suffolks.	Front Line from Q.17.a.1.9. to Q.3.d.9.7.	24th R.W.	Old Reserve Line & AMUSOIRES - HAVERSKERQUE Line S. of inter-battalion boundary.	12th Somersets.
16th Sussex.	Front Line from Q.3.d.9.7. to K.33.b.4.2.	25th R.W.F.	HAMET BILLET.	25th R.W.F.
230th L.T.M.B.	Front Line.	231st L.T.M.B.	- do -	- do -
1 Section 229th L.T.M.B.	- do -	- do -	Rejoin their Bde at HAM-EN-ARTOIS.	- do -

S E C R E T   Copy No.

ADMINISTRATIVE ORDERS

relative to

230th INFANTRY BRIGADE ORDER No.54 of 15-8-18.

15-8-18.

1. TRANSPORT LINES. The 10th Buffs and 15th Suffolks will remain in their present lines.
The 16th Sussex will move with their Unit to HAMET BILLET.

2. BAGGAGE WAGONS of the 16th Sussex will report to their Units Transport Lines at 10 a.m. on the 16th and will rejoin their 449 Coy the same day. Those of other Units will not be required.

3. "B" Teams will remain at the Divisional Reception Camp.

4. TRENCH STORES, AMMUNITION, GRENADES. Units will hand over all Trench Stores, Ammunition, Reserve Ration and Water Dumps and obtain a receipt on the pro forma already issued; these lists will be forwarded to Bde.H.Q. by 4 p.m. 17th.
Special attention must be paid to the handing over of solidified alcohol, charcoal, food containers and 10 pack saddles.

A.S. Campbell Capt,
A/Staff Capt.
230th Infantry Brigade.

Issued at

Copies to:-
Same as for 230th Brigade Order No.54.

SECRET.

AMENDMENT to Relief Table attached to 230th INFANTRY BDE
OPERATION ORDER No.54.

Line 1 should read:-

"230th Bde H.Q. from P.11.a.9.1 relieved by 231st Bde H.Q. to
BUSNES CHATEAU P.31.c.4.5"

[signature]

Major,
Brigade Major,
230th Infantry Brigade.

16th August 1918.

Copies to all recipients
of Bde Order No.54.

SECRET.

Copy No....

230th INFANTRY BRIGADE
BATTLE INSTRUCTIONS No. 2.

16th August 1918.

In amplification of BATTLE INSTRUCTIONS No.1 issued yesterday.

1. The 1st Australian Bde, which is attacking on our right, will up to the 1st objective have the 4th Australian Battalion on its left (O.C. Major Mackenzie). The 3rd Australian Battn will leap-frog on the 1st objective and continue the advance to the second and exploitation objectives (C.O. Major Burrett).

2. Units will detail the following to establish touch at points mentioned:-

(a) THE SUFFOLKS.

i. One section on the right just in rear of 1st objective - sunk road L.4.a.8.4 - with 4th Australian Battn.
ii. One platoon on left 1st objective - sunk road F.28.d.2.0 - with Sussex.
iii. One section L.3.d.9.8 with 4th Australian Battn.

(b) THE BUFFS.

i. 1 section F.29.d.9.0 with 3rd Australian Battn.
ii. 1 platoon on right at 2nd objective A.25.d.2.0 with 3rd Aust.Bn.
iii. 1 platoon on left at 2nd objective F.30.c.1.9 with Somersets.
iv. 1 platoon on right exploitation line A.26.d.5.0.
v. 1 platoon left Exploitation line A.26.d.5.9.

(c) THE SUSSEX.

i. 1 platoon on right 1st objective F.28.d.2.0 with Suffolks.
ii. 1 platoon on left 1st objective F.28.b.3.4 TOINE POST with 231st Brigade.

(d) THE SOMERSETS.

i. 1 platoon on right 2nd objective F.30.c.1.9 with Buffs
ii. 1 platoon on left 2nd objective - BENJAMIN Trench F.29.b.8.9 - with 10th K.S.L.I.
iii. 1 platoon on right Exploitation line A.26.d.5.9
iv. 1 platoon on left " " A.26.b.2.9.

3. Brigade Advance Report Centre and Visual Stations will open as the advance progresses about the following localities:-

(a) F.25.d.7.5.
(b) F.28.d.central.

There will also be a Divisional Visual Station at K.3.central. It will be connected by wire with Div.H.Q. and is for the use of all formations. The call will be "V.S."

4. POWER BUZZERS. Each attacking Brigade will be provided with two complete Loop-Sets, providing communication for 2 Battn H.Q, one Report Centre and one Bde H.Q. Messages can be sent in clear when fighting is in progress at the discretion of C.O's.

5. Pigeons are being supplied to Battalions.

Wbruxton

Major,
Brigade Major,
230th Infantry Brigade.

Issued to Signals at

Same distribution.

SECRET. Copy No...

230th INFANTRY BRIGADE

BATTLE INSTRUCTIONS No.I. 15th August 1918.

Ref.Map - Sheets 62c N.E. & 62b, 1/20,000

1. (a) The 74th Division, in conjunction with 1st Australian Division on right and 58th Division on left, is about to attack and capture the enemy positions forward of the HINDENBURG Line.
(b) Of the 74th Divn, the 230th Inf.Bde on the right and 231st Inf.Bde on left, each reinforced by one Battalion 229th Bde, will deliver the assault.
(c) Of the 230th Inf.Bde, the Suffolks on the right and Sussex on left will lead the attack and capture the GREEN line.
(d) The Buffs on right and Somersets on left will follow the attack, subsequently passing through the Suffolks and Sussex respectively on the Green line and continue the advance to capture and consolidate RED line. Those two Battalions will be prepared subsequently to take advantage of any opportunity - should such favourable situation arise - to push on to the EXPLOITATION line.
(e) Details as to Battalions and Brigades on our flanks will be communicated later.

2. ZERO day and hour will be notified later.

3. (a) The boundaries of the attack for the 230th Inf.Bde are as follows:-
SOUTH boundary:- L.1.d.0.3 - L.2.d.0.3 - L.3.d.0.3 - F.29.c.0.0.
NORTH boundary:- E.29.cent - F.25.cent - F.27.a.9.1 - F.28.b.35.35 - F.29.b.90.85 - A.26.b.00.85.
Inter-BATTALION Boundary:- L.1.a.0.8 - L.3.b.10.8 - F.28.c.10.0 - F.29.c.cent - F.29.d.10.9 - thence due East.
(b) The start line is the present front line, but the Suffolks will start South of the COLOGNE River with right on Sunken Road L.8.a.2.7.
(c) Objective lines are as follows:-
1st objective, GREEN line = L.4.b.9.0 - L.4.b.4.6 - F.28.d.2.0 - CONNOR POST - ~~Stone~~ Joiner Post and continuation of trench system North.
2nd objective, RED line = A.25.d.3.0 - F.30.c.7.8 - F.30.c.3.7 - Rifleman Post - Benjamin Post, etc.
3. Line of EXPLOITATION = A.26.d.central - QUENNEMONT PIT LANE.

4. The attack will be carried out under a barrage supported by moving batteries and a machine gun barrage. Barrage maps will be issued in due course.
Heavy artillery will be engaging enemy batteries and other selected targets.

5. Each Battalion will have ½ section 'A' Coy M.G.Bn attached, and Buffs & Somersets will each also have 2 L.T.M's.

6. The Buffs will take over the portion of the front line now held by the Suffolks in L.1.a & c on X/Y night.

7. Further instructions will follow

8. ACKNOWLEDGE.

Major,
Brigade Major,
230th Infantry Brigade.

Issued to Signals at

Copies to:-
1 10 Buffs
2 15 Suffolks
3 16 Sussex
4 12 Somerset L.I.
5 'A' Coy M.G.Bn.
6 L.T.M.B.
7 44 Bde R.F.A.
8 231 Inf.Bde.
9 ~~2nd~~ 1st Australian Bde.

S E C R E T.   Copy No....

230th INFANTRY BRIGADE ORDER No.55.

21st August 1918.

1. The 74th Division will extend its front on the night 22nd/23rd August to the South grid line of map squares Q.23, Q.24, R.19, R.20, etc Eastwards.
   The Divisional Southern Boundary will then run as shown on attached map.

2. (a) The 231st Infantry Brigade will take over the Outpost System as far South as this new Boundary.
   (b) Completion of relief will be wired to Div.H.Q.
   (c) Command of this portion of the Divisional Front will pass to G.O.C. 74th Division on completion of the Infantry relief.
   (d) The Artillery relief will be arranged direct between C.R.A.s concerned.

3. (a) 230th Infantry Brigade will take over responsibility for the Reserve Line as far South as the new Divisional Boundary.
   The C.R.A. will arrange to cover the new portion of the Reserve Line, which remains the Line of Retention.
   (b) The Reserve Line will be held by a series of nucleus garrisons, consisting of 4 platoons in each Battalion sector. The remainder of the two Battalions now in the Reserve and AMUSOIRES lines will be billeted in ROBECQ and ST FLORIS.

4. The Reserve Line will be garrisoned as follows:-
   Northern Battalion Sector - boundaries as before - by 1 Coy 10 Buffs
   Central Battalion Sector - boundaries from Northern Section P.12.d.7.1. to Q.19.d.5.6 by 2 platoons 10 Buffs and 2 platoons 15 Suffolks - dividing line between Battalions through Q.13.a.7.3.
   Southern Battalion Sector - from Q.19.d.5.6 to Q.26.c.3.5, by one Company 15 Suffolks.

5. The remainder of 10 Buffs and 15 Suffolks, other than the 6 platoons of each remaining in the Reserve line will go into billet in St FLORIS and ROBECQ respectively.

6. Billets in accordance with above will be found by Battalions concerned forthwith.

7. O.C. 'B' Coy M.G.Battn will arrange to redispose his guns in accordance with above orders.

8. O's.C. 10 Buffs and 15 Suffolks will be prepared to man the Reserve line at short notice in case of emergency.

9. Move to be completed by 3 p.m. 22nd instant.

10. Completion of move to be wired to Brigade H.Q.

11. ACKNOWLEDGE.

[signature]
Major,
Brigade Major,
230th Infantry Brigade.

Copies to:-
No. 1 10 Buffs
2 15 Suffolks
3 16 Sussex
4 230 L.T.M.B.
(Tracings attached)
5 B.T.O.
6 R.M.R.E.
7 449 Coy A.S.C.
8 230 Field Amb.
9 74th Division
10 11 Inf.Bde.
11 - 13 War Diary.
14 File.

11th Brigade No. B.M.175.

230th Brigade.

Herewith the folowing:-

Map showing Battle Zone and Old p o sitions for Stokes Mortars 1/5000.
Map showing alternative positions for Stokes.
Map of M.G.po sitions.
Map showing tramways.
Map showing systems . 2

Captain.
Brigade Major,
11th Infantry Brigade.

22.8.18.

II

H.Q. 11 Inf Bde

Above recd.

receipt wired

File

S E C R E T.

Copy No.11

230th INFANTRY BRIGADE ORDER No.56.

21st August 1918.

1. Cancel para.4 ~~and~~ of 230th Infantry Brigade Order No.55 and substitute:-

" The whole of the new Brigade Sector of the Reserve Line from Q.26.c.3.5. to the LYS CANAL at J.36.d.0.4. will now be divided into two Battalion Sectors by a line through Q.13.a.7.3. to P.17.c.6.5.
The Northern Battalion Sector will be held by a nucleus garrison of 4 platoons of 10th Buffs.
The Southern Battalion Sector by a nucleus garrison of 4 platoons of 15th Suffilks.

2. Cancel para. 8 of above Order and substitute:-

"On the command 'MAN BATTLE STATIONS' each of the two Battalion Sectors in the Reserve Line will be manned by 3 Companies each of 10th Buffs and 15th Suffolks.
The remaining Company of each of these Battalions will proceed immediately to the AMUSOIRES - HAVERSKERQUE Line from which they will be prepared to counter-attack to retake any part of the Reserve Line that may have been lost".

(Sgd) I.BUXTON.
Major.
Brigade Major.
230th Infantry Brigade.

Copies to:-

All recipients of Order No.55.

<u>S E C R E T.</u> Copy No. 20.

230th INFANTRY BRIGADE ORDER No.57.

<u>Reference Map</u>. 1:40,000. Sheet 36.a. 23-8-18.

1. The 229th Inf.Bde. will relieve the 231st Inf.Bde. as Advanced Brigade on the night 24th/25th August.
Troops of 229th Inf.Bde. will march early on the 24th and will bivouac for the day in or West of the AMUSOIRES Line preparatory to moving forward to relief that night.

2. On completion of relief the 231st Inf.Bde will become the Brigade in Support and will be distributed as follows:-

Brigade H.Q.	LA HAYE.
One Battalion.	ST FLORIS.
" "	ROBECQ.
" "	Asylum, ST VENANT.

Nucleus garrisons in the Reserve Line will be found as at present by the Support Brigade.

3. 230th Inf.Bde. will move in accordance with attached table.

4. Details of relief will be arranged by C.O's concerned.

5. Units of this Brigade will not move off before 9-30 p.m. and only then if Battns of 229th Inf.Bde. have already moved forward of the AMUSOIRES Line.

6. "B" Teams 230th Inf.Bde. will move to the Reserve Brigade Area on 24th instant.

7. Defence instructions, aeroplane photographs and special maps will be handed over.

8. "C" Coy M.G.Battn. at present holding the Reserve Line will come under the Command of B.G.C.,231st Inf.Bde.

9. Command of Line of Retention will pass to B.G.C., 231st Inf.Bde. at 10 a.m. on 25th.

10. Completion of relief will be wired to present Bde.H.Q. by 10th Buffs and 15th Suffolks.
These Units will also report their arrival in their new billets.

11. Bde.H.Q. will close at present position and re-open at P.7.c. at 10 a.m. on 25th August.

12. ACKNOWLEDGE.

[illegible]
Major,
Brigade Major.
230th Infantry Brigade.

Issued at

Copies to:-

No.1. 10th Buffs.	11. C.R.A. 74th Divn.
2. 15th Suffolks.	12. 229th Inf.Bde.
3. 16th Sussex.	13. 231st Inf.Bde.
4. L.T.M.B.	14. 19th Division.
5. "C" Coy.M.G.Bn.	15. Staff Captain.
6. R.M.R.E.	16. O.C.Signals.
7. 449 Coy.A.S.C.	17. War Diary.
8. B.T.O.	18. " "
9. 230th Fd.Ambce.	19. " "
10. 74th Division.	20. File.

MOVEMENT TABLE.

U N I T.	From.	Relieved by,	To.	At present occupied by
Bde.H.Q.	LA HAYE.	231st Inf.Bde.H.Q.	P.7.c.	No one.
10th Buffs.	Northern Section of Reserve Line & ST FLORIS.	10th K.S.L.I. ~~25th R.W.F.~~	LA PIERRIERE	No one.
15th Suffolks.	Southern Section of Reserve Line & ROBECQ.	25th R.W.F. ~~26th Welsh Regt.~~	BUSNES.	No one.
16th Sussex.	D O N O T M O V E.			
230th L.T.M.B.	D O N O T M O V E.			

SECRET. Copy No. 9.

230th INFANTRY BRIGADE ORDER No.58.

25th August 1918.

Ref: Map SHEET 36a, 1:40,000.

1. The 230th Infantry Brigade will move tomorrow 26th to the neighbourhood of ST HILAIRE at present occupied by 176th Infantry Brigade. The latter will move to billets at present occupied by this Brigade.

2. Units will march in accordance with March Table attached.

3. March Discipline and distances as per pamphlet SS.724 will be strictly adhered to.

4. Hourly halts from 10 minutes to the clock hour till the clock hour will as usual be observed but Units must avoid halting in villages.

5. Transport will march with Battalions.

6. Completion of march will be notified immediately to Brigade H.Q

7. Brigade H.Q. will close at present position at 3 p.m. and reopen at ST HILAIRE, N.5.b.4.1 on arrival.

8. ACKNOWLEDGE.

[signature]

Major,
Brigade Major,
230th Infantry Brigade.

Copies to:-

No.1 10th Buffs
2 15th Suffolks
3 16th Sussex
4 230th L.T.M.B.
5 449 Coy A.S.C.
6 S.S.O.
7 176th Inf.Bde.
8 74th Division.
9 File

M A R C H   T A B L E.

Unit	Starting Point	Time	From	To	Relieved by	Route
15th Suffolks	Road Junction P.31.d.3.7	3.30 p.m.	BUSNES	COTTES	17th Sussex	BUSNES-LILLERS-ST HILAIRE Road
10th Buffs	- do -	4 p.m.	PIERRIERE	LESPESSES	26th R.W.F.	- do -
16th Sussex	- do -	4.30 p.m.	HAMET BILLET	BOURECQ	25th K.Liver-pool Regt.	- do -
230th L.T.M.B.	- do -	4.45 p.m.	- do -	ST HILAIRE	176 L.T.M.B.	- do -
Brigade H.Q.	- do -	4.50 p.m.	P.7.c.	- do -	176 Bde H.Q.	- do -

S E C R E T.

Copy No. 7

ADMINISTRATIVE ORDERS

relative to

230th INFANTRY BRIGADE ORDER No.68 of 25-8-18.

Reference:- 1/40,000 Map.36A.

26th August 1918.

1. TRENCH AND AREA STORES.
All Trench, Area and R.E.Stores (including tip carts and Pontoon in excess of Mob Equipment) will be handed over, receipts being given and taken. List of Special Area Stores shown on reverse. Lists of Stores handed over will be forwarded to this Office.

2. TENTS AND SHELTERS. All tents and shelters in excess of those authorised on the Mobilisation Equipment of Units will be handed over. Brigades, Units and Formations concerned will report to Divisional Headquarters the numbers handed over.

3. AMMUNITION AND SUPPLY DUMPS. All Ammunition, Reserve Rations and Water Dumps will be handed over and statements showing amounts handed over will be forwarded to this Office.

4. AMMUNITION. All Ammunition Echelons will move full.

5. SUPPLIES. Refilling Point on 27th inst will be as follows:-

230th Infantry Brigade Group. ST. HILAIRE at 7 a.m. & 5 p.m.

Rations for consumption on 28th will be drawn in the morning with Train Transport and carried on the man. Those for consumption on 29th inst will be drawn in the afternoon and carried in the Supply Wagons, which will accompany Units.

6. ENTRAINMENT. The Division, less R.A., will be entrained on 28th inst, by Groups - 230th Infantry Brigade Group, including 5th R.M.R.E. Fld.Coy. Divnl.H.Q., Employment Coy. and ½ S.A.A. Section D.A.C. at LILLERS.

7. ACKNOWLEDGE.

Capt.,
Staff Capt.
230th Infantry Brigade.

Issued at

Copies to:- No.1. 10th Buffs.
2. 15th Suffolks.
3. 16th Sussex.
4. 230th L.T.M.B.
5. Brigade Supply Officer.
6. 449 Coy. A.S.C.
7. Brigade Major.
8. File.

LIST OF SPECIAL STORES TO BE HANDED OVER.

Gloves. Leather. 20 pairs.) To be returned to O.O. C.T.
Cotton. 40 pairs.) Corps Stores under G.R.O. 4478.

PACKSADDLERY. 60 Sets.

BOOTS GUM THIGH. prs. 24. To be returned to O.O. C.T.

SERVICE DRESS CLOTHING. for exchange of clothing gassed. Any remaining from this issue to be returned to O.O. C.T.

Jackets. 500. Trousers. 500. Puttees. 500.

ANTI-GAS CLOTHING.

Suits Combination.	Suits Anti-Gas Coats Long.	Suits Anti-Gas Trousers.
800	340	340

All CHAFF CUTTERS, SOYERS STOVES, YUKON PACKS and TARPAULINS WHICH BELONG TO THE CORPS AREA will be handed over.

GRENADE DISCHARGERS. To be returned under G.R.O. 4781.

S E C R E T.   Copy No....11...

ADMINISTRATIVE ORDERS

relative to

230th INFANTRY BRIGADE ORDER No.58 of 25-8-18.

Reference:- 1/40,000 Map 36A.   27th August 1918.

1. STANDING ORDERS. Attention is directed to Divisional Standing Orders for Entrainment and Detrainment. The last para (No.11) of which is hereby cancelled. Particular attention is directed to paras 3 re handing of Entraining States to R.T.O.

2. LOADING & OFF LOADING-PARTIES. O.C. 16th Sussex will detail one Company for loading duties. This Company will travel by Train No.19. O.C. 10th Buffs will detail one Company for off-loading duties. This Company will travel by Train No.1.

3. DIVISIONAL ENTRAINING OFFICER. Lieut.H.BROWN 16th Sussex Regt.

4. ADVANCE PARTIES. Following Advance Parties will proceed by Train No.1. and on arrival at destination they will report to Staff Captain:-

Each Inf.Battn.	1 Officer, 4 Coy.Q.M.S. 1 Representative Bn.H.Q. 1 Batman.
R.M.R.E.	1 Officer, 1 Sergt. 1 Batman.
449 Coy.A.S.C.	1 Supply Officer, 1 N.C.O. 1 Batman.
Field Ambulance.	1 Officer, 1 Sergt, 1 Batman.

1 Bicycle will be taken by each Officer.

5. DETRAINING OFFICERS. The O.C.,the off-loading Coy will act under the A/D.A.A.G.as Divisional Detraining Officer and wire the state of Detrainment in accordance with G.R.O. 4743 dated 11/8/18.
O.C. off-loading Coy will report to Bde.H.Q. at 11 a.m. 28th for instructions.

6. ENTRAINMENT. Units will entrain in accordance with the attached Schedules.

7. SUPPLY AND BAGGAGE WAGONS. Supply and Baggage Wagons of the Divisional Train will be entrained with the Units to which they are affiliated.

8. SUPPLIES. Refilling point on 28th will be ST HILAIRE at 2 p.m. Units will carry rations for consumption 29th on the man and for the 30th on the Supply Wagons.
Units entraining after 12 am on 29th will carry breakfast for 30th on the man.

9. MOTOR TRANSPORT. Motor Lorries as under will be available at Bde.H.Q. at 2 p.m.:-

Each Infantry Battn.	1 Lorry.
L.T.M.B.	1 Lorry.
230th Field Ambulance.	1 Lorry.

Lorries when loaded will return to Bde.H.Q. where they will remain until the morning of the 29th inst when they will proceed to new area by road. No surplus baggage to be taken on the train.
O.C. 15th Suffolks will detail an Officer to take charge of Lorry Convoy, he should report to Bde.H.Q. at 11 a.m. on 28th inst for instructions.

10. DETRAINMENT. 230th Infantry Brigade Group detrain at HEILLY.

11. ACKNOWLEDGE.

Percy Cockerill
Capt,
Staff Capt.
230th Infantry Brigade

Issued at

Copies to:- No.1. 10th Buffs.
2. 15th Suffolks.
3. 16th Sussex.
4. 230th L.T.M.B.
5. 449 Coy.A.S.C.
6. Bde. Supply Officer.
No.7. 230th Field Ambulance.
8. R.M.R.E.
9. 74th Division.
10. S.A.A., Section, D.A.C.
11. Brigade Major.
12. File.

230th INFANTRY BRIGADE GROUP.

ENTRAINING STATION - LILLERS.

Train No.	Marche.	Hour of Depart.	Date.	Contents.
1.	H.T. 72.	22.41.	28/8/18	230th Bde.H.Q. 230th Signal Sec. 230th L.T.H.B. 230th Fd.Ambce. 1 Coy.Cooker & Team of 10th Bn. E.K.Regt. Advce Party 230th Bde.Group, D.H.Q. and Signals.
4.	H.T. 51.	1.41.	29/8/18.	10th Bn.E.K.Regt, less 1 Coy, Cooker and Team.
7.	H.T. 54.	4.41.	29/8/18.	15th Bn.Suffolk Regt. less 1 Coy Cooker and Team.
10.	H.T. 57.	7.41.	29/8/18.	16th Bn.Sussex Regt. less 1 Coy., Cooker and Team.
13.	H.T. 60.	10.41.	29/8/18.	74th Div.H.Q.,H.Q. Emp.Coy. H.Q. & No.1 Sec.Div.Signals. Headquarters R.E.
16.	H.T. 63.	13.41.	29/8/18.	5th Fld.Coy.R.M.R.E. 449 Coy. Div.Train, 1 Coy., Cooker and Team of 15th Bn.Suffolk Regt.
19.	H.T. 66.	16.41.	29/8/18.	½ S.A.A.Sect.74th D.A.C. 1 Coy., Cooker & team of 16th Bn.Sussex. Regt.

Composition of Trains :- 1 Coach, 30 Covereds, 17 Flats.
Transport to be at Station 3 hours before departure of train, personnel 1 hour.

Vol. 6.

Headquarters,
230th Inf. Bde
(74th Division)

September 1918

BRITISH SALONIKA FORCE.

WAR DIARY.

Vol. No.	Unit	Period From	To
41. 42	{ 4th Advanced Park Coy. R.E.	{ 1·3·19 — 1·4·19 —	31·3·19 30·4·19
24.	33rd Base Park Coy. R.E.	29·3·19 —	28-4-19.
28. & 29 —	273rd Railway Construction Coy. R.E.	1-2-19 —	31·3·19.
41.	270th Railway Labour Coy. R.E.	1·4·19	30·4·19
33.	19th Rly. Op. Coy. R.E.	1·4·19	21·4·19.
25.	32nd do do	1·3-19	31·3·19
17.	137th Army Troops Coy. R.E.	1·4·19 —	30·4·19
39	139th Army Troops Coy. R.E.	1·4·19 —	30·4·19
31.	420th West Lancs Field Coy. R.E.	1·4·19	19·4·19

A.P. & S.D., Ska. 1118/1070/1 1000 14/1/19 Pap.

a & Q

61 Division

August

1916

1. 230 Inf Bde HQ 230 Inf Bde

WAR DIARY or ~~INTELLIGENCE SUMMARY.~~

(Erase heading not required.)

Army Form C. 2118.

Instructions regarding War Diaries and Intelligence Summaries are contained in F. S. Regs., Part II. and the Staff Manual respectively. Title pages will be prepared in manuscript.

BEF SEPT 1918 Vol 6

REFMAP 1/20000 62 C N.W.

Place	Date	Hour	Summary of Events and Information	Remarks and references to Appendices
1. A23 cent	1	4 am	The guides supplied by the 47 Div to bivouacs soon lost their way and battns did not arrive in bivouac ~~before~~ at ~~about~~ B20 b&d before about 4.30 am. – BHQ opened at A23 cent	Sheet 62C.N.W. 1/20000
		10 am	BGC attended conference Div HQ. Bde group formed – C Coy MG RMMG. 230 F Amb – Bde to form Support Bde.	
		6.30 pm	BHQ closed at "Y" wood and opened at B26 d 2 6 7.15 pm.	
		8.15 pm	BGC called up all COs, & gave them orders with view to following situations (a) To support 229 Inf Bde who are attacking (b) In the event of 2nd Australian Div being behind 229 I.B. to form supporting flank along refused right flank.	
			16 Sussex the latter detailed to undertake (b) scheme.	
C25 b 4 2	2		During the night Bns moved to positions of assembly arriving by 5.30 am – BHQ moved to C25 b 4 2.	
		5.30 am	16 Sussex maintained touch with 229th Inf Bde when they attacked at 5.30 am & with Australians on the right. When 229 Inf Bde eventually returned after suffering considerable casualties to their jumping off trenches 16 Sussex remained up East of HOWE & ALLAINES linking up the two divisions.	

[signature] Major, BM. 230 Inf Bde

D. D. & L., London, E.C. (A8004) Wt. W1771/M2031 750,000 5/17 Sch. 52 Forms/C2118/14

2

230 INF BDE

BEF

WAR DIARY
or
INTELLIGENCE SUMMARY.

(*Erase heading not required.*)

SEPT 1918

Army Form C. 2118.

Instructions regarding War Diaries and Intelligence Summaries are contained in F. S. Regs., Part II. and the Staff Manual respectively. Title pages will be prepared in manuscript.

Place	Date	Hour	Summary of Events and Information	Remarks and references to Appendices
C25 b [illegible]	2		16 Sussex in very exposed position overlooked from AIZECOURT and could not move about. Rations did not reach 16 Sussex, owing to guides not turning up. During the night 10 Buffs and 15 Suffolks relieved 229 Bde in SCUTARI and BROUSSA trenches. Suffolks with their right on 16 Sussex, 10 Buffs on left of 15 Suffolks, with their left joining 47 Div in C.16 b.c The following casualties occurred during the day, principally from shell fire. 10 Buffs 1 OR killed 1 OR wounded. 15 Suffs 2 -do- 16 -do- 16 Sussex 12 -do- 2 off. wounded & 28 OR –	MAP 1:20000 62C NW
	3.	9.30 am	Australians ordered to relieve 16 Sussex, but both Aust: the Cmdr OC Sussex agree that it would be impossible to relieve them by daylight, so postponed till after dark. Patrols were pushing by all means as there are indications of the enemy withdrawing. In case of advance. Advanced Guard Brigade formed as follows. 230 Inf Bde. 1 Sqdn Northumberland Hussrs. 117 Bde RFA. 1 Sect RMRE 1 Sect 253 Tunnelling Co. Divisional boundaries E & W line through E 29 Cent. Right and dividing line through C11 c 7 continued eastwards left boundary	
		1.45 pm	Enemy still reported holding MIDINETTE trench by patrols. After dark Sussex withdrew to C 26 C. During the day [illegible] [illegible] patrols were carried out by 16 Sussex.	
			[illegible] Major BM 230 Inf Bde	

D. D. & L., London, E.C.
(A8004) Wt. W1771/M2031 750,000 5/17 Sch. 52 Forms/C2118/14

3.

230 INF BE

B.E.F.

Instructions regarding War Diaries and Intelligence Summaries are contained in F. S. Regs., Part II. and the Staff Manual respectively. Title pages will be prepared in manuscript.

WAR DIARY
or
INTELLIGENCE SUMMARY.
(Erase heading not required.)

Sept 1918

Army Form C. 2118.

Place	Date	Hour	Summary of Events and Information	Remarks and references to Appendices
C25b42	3.		Casualties reported today as follows:-	Map 1:20000 62c N.W.
			10 Buffs 1 O.R. wounded	
			15 Suffolks 3 -do-	
			16 Sx 1 O.R. killed 10 -do-	
	4	9AM	BGC attended conference at DHQ.	
			Patrols report MIDINETTE Trench D19d occupied by enemy still.	
		pm	Orders issued for attack on enemy line to be carried out 5-45 am tomorrow under a barrage. This scheme was cancelled owing to enemy front trench being evacuated.	
			Casualties today 10 Buffs 14 OR wounded 16 Sussex 2 officers wounded 16 OR wounded	
	5	11.30am	15 Suffolks sideslipped to the right and passed through 231 Inf Bde.	
		11.40 am	and pushed on together with the Buffs arrived in MIDINETTE Trench	
		12.30 pm	and pushing on to PERONNE-NURLU Rd in D20.	
J1a4.5		5.45 pm	Buffs report enemy concentrating in D2c. Artillery turned on. Advanced report centre opened at J1a4.8. BHQ to huts in I6 central.	
		6.25pm	Suffolks in line J9a73 to D27b73. Buffs moved in trench D13d under M.G. fire & conformed to Suffolks. 16 Sussex (Support) to MIDINETTE Trench left flank of Buffs considerably N. of Div boundary to keep touch with Left Division. Right flank of Bde had been protected by 25 RWF 231 Inf Bde, especially situated as Australians were not up in line.	

[illegible] Major
230 Inf Bde

D. D. & L., London, E.C. (A8001) Wt. W1771/M2031 750,000 5/17 Sch. 52 Forms/C2118/14

4

230 Inf Bde

BEF

Instructions regarding War Diaries and Intelligence Summaries are contained in F. S. Regs., Part II. and the Staff Manual respectively. Title pages will be prepared in manuscript.

WAR DIARY
or
INTELLIGENCE SUMMARY.
(*Erase heading not required.*)

Sept 1918

Army Form C. 2118.

Place	Date	Hour	Summary of Events and Information	Remarks and references to Appendices
D16 a 4.5	5		During the day 9 prisoners were captured by the Buffs	Map 1:20000 62c NE
	6		~~Casualties inflicted were [illegible]~~	
	6	8 am	After bombardment of Templeux Trench advance continued without much	
		8.45 am	opposition and first objective Templeux trench was taken. The advance	
		2 pm	continued until at 2.35 pm the opposition in front of the Buffs increased.	
		6 pm	By 6 pm final objective reached by both Bns. though Suffks were not quite on Div. boundary owing to the features of the terrain.	
			During the day 3 prisoners by Suffolks were taken. Some casualties were caused to the enemy though probably not a large number.	
	7	am	231 Bde went thro 230 Bde who came into support) except 16 Sussex who formed defensive flank on left of 231 Bde.	
Templeux la Fosse		4 pm	BHQ went into old British huts at Templeux la Fosse.	
			During these operations the weather has been fine and warm.	
			Casualties Buffs 2 OR killed 1 Offr wounded 12 O.R. wounded	
			Suffk 2 " 1 " 14 " 6 missing (prob. killed)	
			Sussex — — 10.	
	8		No move - Weather windy & raining.	
	9		Showers and wind. Half Bde salvaging back areas during afternoon	
	10		Rain & wind all night.	
	11		9 pm BHQ moved to D30 b 7.7 where Nissen huts are being put up.	
	12		During 10/11th 16 Sussex relieved 16 Devons on right of the line; Buffs [illegible] RH. Suffolks in support relieved Somersets relief complete 1.30 am.	
			Skinner [?]	

J Thurston [?] Major
BM 230 Inf Bde

D. D. & L., London, E.C. (A8001) Wt. W1771/M2031 750,000 5/17 Sch. 52 Forms/C2118/14

5

230 Inf Bde
BEF

Instructions regarding War Diaries and Intelligence Summaries are contained in F. S. Regs., Part II. and the Staff Manual respectively. Title pages will be prepared in manuscript.

WAR DIARY
or
INTELLIGENCE SUMMARY.
(Erase heading not required.)

Sept 1918

Army Form C. 2118.

Place	Date	Hour	Summary of Events and Information	Remarks and references to Appendices
D30b77.	12		Stormy.	Ref map 1/20000 62 C NE
		8.50pm	16 Sussex having observed Germans in BOULEUX WOOD, put out L.G. post to catch them approaching.	
		8.55pm	Strong enemy patrol turned up at 8.55 pm. L.G. jammed and our party had to retire under determined bombing attack. Cpl. + 1 man covered retirement with bombs. Casualties were caused amongst the enemy.	
	13	11am	Windy + showery. 11 a.m. Conference at Div HQ of B.G.C.	
		10.30pm	x Two hostile bombing planes caught in our searchlights and shot down by one of our planes.	
	14.		Divisional front from tonight held by two Bdes. Dismount 24 W.R. (231 Bde) relieved 10 Buffs on the left, who came into Reserve, on main line of resistance. 15 Suffolks relieved the right of 16 Sussex. The new Bde front held by 15 Suffolks and 16 Sussex. Relief complete 11.50 pm.	
			x The pilot from one of these planes came down just in front of 16 Sussex in parachute and was captured.	
	15		During the evening + early night some shelling in neighbourhood of [illegible] and road close by.	
		1030pm	Enemy bombing machine shot down.	
	16.	7pm	After dusk 16 Sussex sidestepped to the right handing over a small piece of the line to 231 Bde + taking over a small piece from ~~16 Sussex~~ 15 Suffolks. 10 Buffs moved to position of assembly between FAUSTINE QUARRY + K.S.B. cent.	

[illegible] for Brigade Major 230 Inf Bde

D. D. & L., London, E.C. (A8001) Wt. W1771/M2031 750,000 5/17 Sch. 52 Forms/C2118/14

6-

Instructions regarding War Diaries and Intelligence Summaries are contained in F. S. Regs., Part II. and the Staff Manual respectively. Title pages will be prepared in manuscript.

230 Inf Bde
BEF

WAR DIARY
or
INTELLIGENCE SUMMARY.
(Erase heading not required.)

Sept 1918

Army Form C. 2118.

Place	Date	Hour	Summary of Events and Information	Remarks and references to Appendices
D30b77	16		12 Somersets (229 Bde) placed under orders of BGC 230 Inf Bde & moved to position of assembly between KOBCAMP & SPUR QUARRY.	Ref map 1:20000 62 C NE
		9.45pm	Enemy bombing machines hit 2 ammunition lorries just west of LONGAVESNES causing repeated explosions, also struck Sussex Transport killing 7 men and 6 animals & wounding 13 men and 3 animals, & afterwards bombed 12 Somersets Transport killing 6 animals (5 chargers) & wounding 13 other animals.	
			During the night there was heavy gas shelling in the valley of concentration especially on Somersets who had 90 men evacuated.	
	17	1am	Very heavy thunderstorm.	
			For ensuing operations following troops attached to Bde: 1 Troop Northumberland Hussars A Coy M.G. Bn. 1 Sect 182 Tunnelling Co for booby traps. 1 Sect RMRE	
			During the night 15 Suffolks moved two Coys S. of Div boundary (COLOGNE RIVER) to attack TEMPLEUX and TEMPLEUX QUARRIES from S.W.	
			Dispositions as follows attacking Bns 15 Suffolks right - 16 Sussex left supported by 10 Buffs & 12 Somersets respectively. 1 Sect M.G. attached each attacking Bn.	
	18	5.20am	Raining & misty - 5.20 am advance began both attacking and support moved off well closed up under our barrage - Barrage 100x to 3 mins at first	

D. D. & L., London, E.C. (A8001) Wt. W1771/M2031 750,000 5/17 Sch. 52 Forms/C2118/14

[illegible]

7

230 Inf Bde

BEF

WAR DIARY
or
INTELLIGENCE SUMMARY.
(*Erase heading not required.*)

Sept 1918

Army Form C. 2118.

Instructions regarding War Diaries and Intelligence Summaries are contained in F. S. Regs., Part II. and the Staff Manual respectively. Title pages will be prepared in manuscript.

Place	Date	Hour	Summary of Events and Information	Remarks and references to Appendices
D30b77	18	5.20am	later it changed to 100x in 4 mins. First objective taken at 7.45 am. The second objective was the old British front line. This was also quickly occupied in places and one Coy at least of 10th Bn. who had leapfrogged Buffs at first objective when barrage remained for the 20 mins nearly reached the Blue line, the old support line of the Hindenburg line but were unable to remain there and unfortunately, in falling back came under a barrage & suffered casualties. Capt. H. Alfrey 10th Buffs was killed about the furthest limit of the Buffs advance. Meanwhile the Sussex who had leapfrogged 16 Sussex on first objective were held up before reaching the Red line, partly owing to the unit on their left being unable to get forward, but eventually about 2 pm the Red line was completely occupied. Between 7 & 800 prisoners were taken by the Bde though some of these found their way to the cages of the Corps on our right. Also 2 batts British field guns & 1, 4.5" How[itzer] and also a German mountain gun were captured. Also many TMs & at least 50 MGs. The two Coys Suffolks detailed to mop up TEMPLEUX & the QUARRIES took over 200 prisoners and did good work in rushing MGs in Templeux who were inconveniencing the Australians attacking on our right	Ref map 1:20000 62c NE

[illegible]

D. D. & L., London, E.C. (A8004) Wt. W1771/M2'31 750,000 5/17 Sch. 52 Forms/C2118/14

9.

Instructions regarding War Diaries and Intelligence Summaries are contained in F. S. Regs., Part II. and the Staff Manual respectively. Title pages will be prepared in manuscript.

230 Inf Bde

B.E.F.

WAR DIARY
or
INTELLIGENCE SUMMARY.

(Erase heading not required.)

Sept 1918

Army Form C. 2118.

Place	Date	Hour	Summary of Events and Information	Remarks and references to Appendices
The Quarries	19.		Cold night with showers –	Ref map 1:20000 62c NE
		5.15 am	S.O.S. sent up from the right of the Division on our left. Div and Bde our barrage was put down, but nothing occurred on our front.	
		7 pm	12 Somersets withdrawn from front line and sent to 229 Inf Bde. at FAUSTINE QUARRIES replaced in front line by 16 Sussex. 15 Suffolks in support.	
		11 pm	B.G.C. called to conference at D.H.Q.	
			Plans changed, instead of being relieved night of 20/21 we are to attack. Average rifle strength of Bns 340 O.R.	
			Casualties for last 24 hours 1 O.R. killed 18 wounded in all Bns.	
	20	9.30 am	Fine night – 9.30 am conference of COs at B.H.Q. explaining programme. Attack to be made tomorrow to our front to take QUADRILATERAL TRENCH	
		7.30 pm	During the evening units assumed positions of assembly on ... road facing N.E. Buffs on the right Sussex on the left. Suffolks occupied posts in our old front line.	
			Casualties during the day 1 O.R. killed 18 wounded in all.	
			Our present trench strength as follows	
			10 Buffs 13 Offrs 370 O.R.	
			15 Suffolks 17 " 367 "	
			16 Sussex 18 " 301 "	

[illegible] Major
Bde Major 230 Inf Bde

D. D. & L., London, E.C.
(A8004) Wt. W1771/M2031 750,000 5/17 Sch. 52 Forms/C2118/14

10

230 Inf Bde

BEF

WAR DIARY
or
INTELLIGENCE SUMMARY.
(Erase heading not required.)

Sept. 1918

Army Form C. 2118.

Instructions regarding War Diaries and Intelligence Summaries are contained in F. S. Regs., Part II. and the Staff Manual respectively. Title pages will be prepared in manuscript.

Place	Date	Hour	Summary of Events and Information	Remarks and references to Appendices
TEMPLEUX QUARRIES	21		Quiet night with fine clear morning -	Ref map 1/20000 62C NE
			The objective for todays Operations was the "Blue Line" i.e. the outpost line of the main HINDENBURG line, including QUENNEMONT FARM and TOMBOIS from A20 c8.1 to A14 C13. The 231 Bde attacked on our left and one Bn of the Australians on our right worked forward to assist our right. But there was necessarily a large gap on our right as it was inadvisable to cross the valley in A25 d and 26 d as it was hopelessly overlooked from the Ridge north and south of MALAKOFF wood -	
		5.40 am	At 5.40 am the barrage came down and after 3 mins moved forward at the rate of 100x in 4 mins - The enemy quickly put down a barrage on our jumping off line which delayed the rear Companies of the Buffs but they quickly followed on - The progress was rapid until the wire of a ZOO trench running parallel to and about 250 yards from TOP Trench was reached - This wire of which anything in front of the Buffs there was more than one belt proved a serious obstacle - meanwhile during the advance the Sussex captured ~~#~~ 98 prisoners including 4 officers in the neighbourhood of QUENNET but unfortunately ~~as~~ the Kiss Cross or QUENNET High trench immediately S of it was not satisfactorily mopped up and ~~[illegible]~~ the machine guns quickly	
			When (?) (?) more,	

D. D. & L., London, E.C.
(A8003) Wt. W1771/M2031 750,000 5/17 Sch. 52 Forms/C2118/14

11.

230 Inf Bde

BEF

Instructions regarding War Diaries and Intelligence Summaries are contained in F. S. Regs., Part II. and the Staff Manual respectively. Title pages will be prepared in manuscript.

WAR DIARY
or
INTELLIGENCE SUMMARY.
(*Erase heading not required.*)

Sept 1918.

Army Form C. 2118.

Place	Date	Hour	Summary of Events and Information	Remarks and references to Appendices
TEMPLEUX QUARRIES	21		opened on our advancing Bns from their left was causing heavy casualties – heavy machine gun fire was also coming from the "QUADRILATERAL" formed by CAT POST and MILL LANE on our left this also greatly inconvenienced our advance and caused casualties. These posts should have been taken by the Bde on our left but had been [illegible]. Also on the right flank heavy machine gun fire came from the [illegible] of [illegible] in MALAKOFF COPSE and from the high ground [illegible] of [illegible] FARM. The casualties caused by all this MG fire made our advancing troops very weak and Capt. F.C. HATFIELD Comdg a leading Coy of the [illegible] was killed. [illegible] a [illegible] of men from the Brigade on our left crossed us and became mixed up with both our leading Bns which apparently caused a gap to be formed on our left flank in the [illegible] VALLEY.	Ref Map 1/20000 62c NE
		6.30 am	The advanced Bns [illegible] in and [illegible] of 200 [illegible]. And [illegible] heavy artillery fire from their right and MG fire from the [illegible] was opened on them forcing them to take cover in shell holes. And the [illegible] [illegible]	

D. D. & L., London, E.C.
(A8004) Wt. W1771/M2 31 750,000 5/17 Sch. 52 Forms/C2118/14

12

230 Inf Bde

BEF

Sept 1918

WAR DIARY
or
INTELLIGENCE SUMMARY.
(Erase heading not required.)

Army Form C. 2118.

Instructions regarding War Diaries and Intelligence Summaries are contained in F. S. Regs., Part II. and the Staff Manual respectively. Title pages will be prepared in manuscript.

Place	Date	Hour	Summary of Events and Information	Remarks and references to Appendices
TEMPLEUX QUARRIES	21		Coys of the Buffs were unable to get forward to reinforce the leading Coys. After 3 Patrols were sent out to try and find a way up to them but all three patrols were wiped out. At the same time the leading Coys tried to send back runners but all of these (3) at once became casualties.	Ref map 1/20000 62C NE
		12.30 pm	The leading troops retained their position till 12.30 pm i.e. 8 hours – at this time the two leading Coys of 16 Sussex numbered in all 40. A strong counter attack was now launched by the enemy on our left flank & left rear from QUENNET COPSE and the leading troops were cut off – this counter attack released considerably over 100 prisoners who had been captured by the 16th Bn and also made the position of our leading troops impossible and a retirement was made to our jumping off line. In many cases hand to hand fighting took place and Capt LASCELLES Coy 16 Sussex is said to have bayonetted 40 enemy on the way back. Capt LASCELLES had been wounded twice early in the morning. This Coy arrived back 28 strong which turned out to be the strongest Coy of the Sussex. Lewis guns covered the retreat of the [illegible] and in the case of the Sussex many of these were [illegible]. [illegible] to the end.	

[illegible] Major

D. D. & L., London, E.C. (A3004) Wt. W1771/M2 31 750,000 5/17 Sch. 52 Forms/C2118/14

13 230 Inf Bde B.E.F

Instructions regarding War Diaries and Intelligence Summaries are contained in F. S. Regs., Part II. and the Staff Manual respectively. Title pages will be prepared in manuscript.

WAR DIARY
or
INTELLIGENCE SUMMARY.
(Erase heading not required.)

Sept. 1918

Army Form C. 2118.

Place	Date	Hour	Summary of Events and Information	Remarks and references to Appendices
TEMPLEUX QUARRIES	21	1250	The Support Bn was unable to render the attacking Bns much assistance in the attack beyond covering a general retirement to the jumping off place which became necessary. The Buffs and Sussex being very disorganised –	
			When the 15 Suffolks were ordered forward to support the attack the 14 RH (229 Inf Bde) were placed under the orders of BGC 230 Inf Bde and occupied the position occupied previously by 15 Suffolks.	
		2pm	On arrival at the Red line the Bde was disposed in the line of defence as follows: 10 Buffs on right in touch with the Australians 15 Suffolks in centre 14 RH on left 16 Sussex in support at TEMPLEUX SWITCH	
		5pm	Redisposition as follows:- 10 Buffs were withdrawn into reserve in SHERWOOD TRENCH and BOLSOVER SWITCH. Buffs in all Coys numbered about 80 16 Sussex numbered about 40 in the Coys.	
	22		Weather showery many more men of Buffs and Sussex came in.	
			The Bns suffered following casualties	
			10 Buffs 6 Offrs 160 OR.	
			15 Suffolks — 50 OR	
			16 Sussex 7 Offrs 160 OR	
	22/23		The Bde was relieved in the line less 15 Suffolks by 229 Inf Bde our Bns occupied Green line	

[illegible signature]

(A7092). Wt. W12839/M1293. 750,000. 1/17. D. D. & L., Ltd. Forms/C.2118/14.

14

Instructions regarding War Diaries and Intelligence Summaries are contained in F. S. Regs., Part II. and the Staff Manual respectively. Title pages will be prepared in manuscript.

230 Inf Bde
BEF

WAR DIARY
or
~~INTELLIGENCE SUMMARY.~~
(~~Erase heading not required.~~)

Sept 1918

Army Form C. 2118.

Place	Date	Hour	Summary of Events and Information	Remarks and references to Appendices
TEMPLEUX QUARRIES	23.	9pm	While at mess shell struck mess hut wounded Bde Staff Capt, Bde Int. Offr, Bde Sig Offr, Bde Gas Offr, Mess Capt. Bde Maj. wounded very slightly, remaining at duty; all remainder evacuated. Lt Col RALSTON 10th Buffs called in to command Bde. Capt Blunt 16 Hussars called in as Staff Capt.	
	24.	9am	Lt Col H.T.P. EDWARDS 16 Hussars arrived and took over command of the Bde from 8 Team.	
		7.30pm	Bde less 15th Suffks moved into bivouac west of LONGAVESNE. BHQ 230 b 55	
		9pm	Transport ~~lines~~ less cookers and L.G. limbers started by road to destination to FOUILLOY.	
	25.	7.30am	Bde group less 15th Suffks marched to PERONNE and entrained 12N for VILLERS BRETONNEUX and marched to billets as below.	
			BHQ FOUILLOY; 15th Suffks " rejoined Bde.; 10th Buffs AUBIGNY; 16 Sx FOUILLOY; 230 TMB "; L.T.M.B. "; RMRE AUBIGNY; 74 M G Bn "; 447 Coy ASC "	
		10.30am	Cookers and L.G. limbers went by road in Div convoy.	
	26.	12.30pm	First line transport convoy arrived and parked at AUBIGNY	
		3pm	2nd transport convoy arrived.	
			Lt W.L. MERRICK arrived and took over duties of Signal Officer.	

D. D. & L., London, E.C.
(A8004) Wt. W1771/M2 31 750,000 5/17 Sch 52 Forms/C2118/14

Buxton Major
Bde Maj 230 Inf Bde

-15-

230 Inf Bde

BEF

Instructions regarding War Diaries and Intelligence Summaries are contained in F. S. Regs., Part II. and the Staff Manual respectively. Title pages will be prepared in manuscript.

WAR DIARY
or
~~INTELLIGENCE SUMMARY.~~
(Erase heading not required.)

Sept 1918

Army Form C. 2118.

Place	Date	Hour	Summary of Events and Information	Remarks and references to Appendices
Fouilloy	27		Bde started moving to V Army Area at LILLERS, in following order. Entraining station LILLERS.	
			Bde HQ. T.M.B. & L.T.M.B.	
			10th Buffs	
			15th Suffolks	
			[illegible] Co ASC	
			RMRE CRASC	
			74 M.G. Bn	
			16 Sussex	
	28	[illegible]	First train arrived LILLERS reached billets at ALLOUAGNE at [illegible] pm.	
Allouagne			Units billeted as below	
			Bde HQ. L.T.M.B. 10th Buffs 15th Suffolks ALLOUAGNE	
			16 Sussex L'ECLEME RMRE HAUTE RIEUX	
			74 M.G. Bn BUSNETTES F.A. BOIS DES DAMES	
			All trains after the first two arrived very late. 16 Sussex did not arrive till [illegible] on 29th. They should have arrived [illegible] evening.	
	29		Lt Col. C.J.H. SPENCE-JONES DSO. 24 WR arrived and assumed command of the Bde.	
	30		Wet and cold. Warning order to relieve 58th Division in the line. Advanced parties [illegible] to take over by lorry.	
			Strength. This became very weak after foregoing operations and received only following drafts [illegible] since 21st Sept. 10th Buffs 8 offrs 87 OR. 15th Suffolks 1 offr 75 OR. 16 Sussex 3 offrs 21 OR. Making following ~~[illegible]~~ trench strengths totals[?] 10 Buffs 18 off 385 OR 15 Suffolks 18 offs 444 OR 16 Sussex 17 offrs 259 OR.	
				[illegible] Capt. Bde Maj. 230 Inf Bde

D. D. & L., London, E.C.
(A8004) Wt. W1771/M2731 750,000 5/17 Sch. 52 Forms/C2118/14

SECRET.

With reference to Brigade Order No.67, "Z" Day will be the 18th September.

The hour of Zero will be notified at 1 p.m. on "Y" day.

ACKNOWLEDGE.

Major,
Brigade Major,
230th Infantry Brigade.

16th September 1918.

Distribution same as for Bde Order.

SECRET.

Copy No. 8...

230th INFANTRY BRIGADE ORDER No.67.

~~16th August~~ Sept 1918.

1. In continuation of 230th Infantry Bde BATTLE INSTRUCTIONS Nos 1 & 2
x already issued.
2. The 38th German Division with 96th, 95th and 94th Infantry Regts from right to left is believed to be holding the front opposite to 74th Divn.
3. The following will be attached to the Brigade for these operations:-
   (a) ½ troop Northumberland Hussars for intercommunication.
   (b) 1 section R.M.R.E.
   (c) Detachment Tunnelling Co with knowledge of forward area.
   (d) 'A' Coy 74th M.G.Bn (less 2 sections).
4. DISTRIBUTION OF TROOPS. The assembly area allotted to the Brigade is that East of a North and South line through K.4 central and the Brigade will take over its attacking front on X/Y night.
   The 229th Brigade (less 2 Battalions) with one M.G.Coy will be in Divisional Reserve and will be locatedabout FAUSTINE QUARRY in K.5.d.0.0 on Y/Z night.
   Accordingly on night 16/17th the following movements will take place:-
   SUSSEX - hand over front line N of F.25 central to 231st Bde and take over from Suffolks as far South as L.1.a.8.8.
   BUFFS - move to preliminary position of assembly in area between Southern edge FAUSTINE QUARRY and K.5.b central.
   SOMERSETS - move to preliminary position of assembly in area between K.5.b central and SPUR QUARRY.
   On night of 17/18th:-
   BUFFS take over from Suffolks from L.1.a.8.8 to L.1.c.4.4.
   SUFFOLKS take over from 1st Australian Divn from L.8.a.0.0 to L.1.d.6.0 and West of that line in trench system L.7.a.
5. METHOD OF ATTACK on Z DAY.
   (a) At Zero hour minus 30 minutes all troops holding the front systems will move forward and form up and lie down on a line 300 yards West of the barrage line. Wire in front of trenches to be cut in sufficient places to admit of this being done expeditiously and the forming-up line to be taped previous to forming up.
   At the same hour the Somersets will occupy the front trenches vacated by the Sussex and the area immediately West.
   The Buffs will similarly close up their rear Companies to occupy the trenches vacated by their front companies.
   (b) At Zero hour + 3, when the barrage first lifts, the whole will advance simultaneously.
   (c) The Suffolks will attack TEMPLEUX LE GUERARD and the Quarries East of it moving in an E.N.E. direction in close cooperation with the 4th Australian Battn which will attack BOLSOVER SWITCH in L.4.c. The Suffolks will detail one company to mop up TEMPLEUX LE GUERARD and 1 company to mop up the Quarries in L.3.a & b while the other two Coys push on to the 1st objective and consolidate.
   (d) The Sussex will attack Eastwards to the 1st objective on the frontage allotted, detiling if found necessary 2 platoons to assist in mopping up the Quarries North of L.3.b.0.7.
   (e) 1 section M.G's will be attached to each of these attacking Battalions and will cover the advance to the 1st objective. These sections will subsequently move up to 1st objective, will assist in consolidation thereof and will cover with their fire the area between the 1st and 2nd objectives.
   (f) THE BUFFS will advance to the 1st objective North of TEMPLEUX LE GUERARD (in L.2.b) and along Northern slopes of Quarries Spur General line F.27.d central. The Battalion is not to follow the barrage but will halt in any locality found suitable about 27.c & d until such time as will admit of its reaching the 1st objective line - Connor Post (inclusive) to South Divisional boundary) - in time to advance behind barrage to 2nd objective.
   (g) THE SOMERSETS will follow in support of the Sussex, but at a gradually increasing distance, and will halt in valley F.26.d.3.5 and Northwards or other suitable locality until such time as will admit of its reaching the ~~N~~ 1st objective line - Connor Post (exclusive) to Northern Brigade boundary - in time to advance behind barrage to 2nd objective.
   (h) The O.C. 230 L.T.M.B. will arrange to send forward 2 Stokes Mortars to assist in defence of RED line as soon as captured.

6. Objective lines gained will be consolidated and the defence organised in depth. In view of the enemy having probably registered the existing trench systems, troops should, when possible, dig in on lines some 300 yards in advance of old systems. Each platoon will fire a Green Very light on reaching the 1st objective (Green line) and a Red Very Light on reaching the 2nd objective (Red line).
The barrage will come down at Zero on the North and South grid line between F.25 and F.26 as far South as the COLOGNE River.
The 1st Australian Div. barrage line runs from L.2.c.0.3 to L.8.a.5.0.

7. LINE OF EXPLOITATION (Blue Line).
When the 2nd objective line has been taken and consolidation is proceeding, every effort will be made by the Buffs and Somersets to establish posts on the Blue line, and by the former especially to secure MALAKOFF WOOD SPUR in A.26.d.
Certain batteries will be moving forward so soon as the Red line has been secured and will be prepared to cover posts established on the Blue line.

8. SECRECY. The necessity for secrecy is impressed on all concerned. Reconnaissance is to be reduced to a minimum and no reference to these operations is to be made on the telephone.

9. CAPTURED GUNS. In the event of capture of enemy guns, information to be sent to Brigade H.Q. for transmission to the Artillery, giving exact location of guns, nature of gun and whether ammunition is at hand. Spare parts, sights etc are not to be removed as souvenirs.

10. ROADS.
The VILLERS FAUCON - TEMPLEUX - RONSSOY is allotted for use.

11. AEROPLANES.
(a) A contact aeroplane will fly over the front at:-
Zero+ 2 hours 15 minutes.
Zero+ 5 hours.
Zero+ 7 "
and subsequently as ordered.
Troops to be warned to be on the look-out for these 'planes and to indicate their positions by means of flares, rifles in rows of 3, and waving of helmets. Red flares only will be used.
Brigade and Battalion H.Q. will display their Ground Signal Sheets and Strips when our aeroplanes are flying over.
(b) A counter-attack plane will be up continuously from daylight onwards with the sole mission of detecting approach of enemy counter-attacks. This 'plane will fly in the direction of any observed counter-attack dropping a white parachute flare as near to the counter-attacking troops as possible.

12. S.O.S. SIGNAL is
RED over RED over RED.

13. TIME. An Officer from each Unit will attend at Brigade H.Q. about 2 p.m. and 6.30 p.m. on Y day to synchronise watches. Synchronisation is not to be carried out by telephone.

14. Brigade H.Q. will open at sunken road E.28.b.2.0 at Zero hour.

15. Barrage tables will be issued later.

16. ACKNOWLEDGE.

[signature]
Major,
Brigade Major,
230th Infantry Brigade.

Issued to Signals at

Same distribution as for BATTLE INSTRUCTIONS.

SECRET. Copy No. 8...

230th INFANTRY BRIGADE
BATTLE INSTRUCTIONS No.3.

16th ~~August~~ September 1918.

The following will be the Artillery and Machine Gun barrage arrangements on Z day:-

1. ARTILLERY.
230th Inf.Bde will be covered by a group formed of 44th and 104th F.A. Bdes under Lt.Col C.C.ROBERTSON D.S.O. who will send a liaison Officer not below the rank of Captain to 230th Brigade H.Q.

The attack will be carried out under the protection of
(a) a creeping Field Artillery barrage.
(b) Heavy artillery back barrage.
(c) Machine Gun barrage.

There will be no preliminary bombardment on Z day. The lifts of the barrage (which will always be 100 yards) will be at the following times:-

First lift (from barrage start line)	0+3
Second lift	0+5
Third lift	0+8

and so on in three minute lifts till the eleventh lift at 0+32.

The twelfth and all subsequent lifts of the barrage will be at the rate of 100 yards in 4 minutes, i.e.

Twelfth lift	0+36
Thirteenth lift	0+40

and so on.

There will be a halt on the GREEN line of over an hour, and the barrage will commence to creep from the GREEN line at Zero+3 hours and 10 minutes and continue at the rate of 100 yards in four minutes to the RED line. The barrage will thicken up three minutes before the advance to warn the troops of the lift.

On lifting off the 2nd objective the barrage will remain as a protective barrage for 15 minutes and will then die away.

The S.O.S barrage will be arranged in the first instance to cover the RED line but will be moved forward to cover the BLUE line should the exploitation prove successful.

2. MACHINE GUNS.
(a) Barrage to cover advance from Starting line to line N and S through F.27 central will be carried out by 2 Companies 2nd Life Guards M.G.Bn. On completion 1 Company will remain in or about old Front line as garrison Remaining Company will be withdrawn to Divisional Reserve.
(b) Barrage for advance from 1st objective (GREEN line) to 2nd objective (RED line) will be carried out by two sections A Coy, D Coy and two Sections C Coy 74th M.G.Battn. On completion 2 sections A Coy and 2 sections C Coy will undertake consolidation West of and including 1st objective. D Coy will remain on or about 1st objective but will be disposed in depth. All these guns will be prepared to put down S.O.S barrage in front of 2nd objective in emergency.
(c) Advance from line N and S through F.27 central to the 1st objective will be covered by direct overhead fire of two sections of each of A and C Companies allotted to 230th and 231st Brigades respectively. These Sections under the orders of B.G's.C will also be responsible for the consolidation of ground between 1st and 2nd objectives.
(d) After "Stand to" on Z+1 day, unless otherwise ordered, D Coy will revert to Divisional Reserve and whole of A Coy and whole of C Coy to 230th and 231st Inf.Bdes respectively.
(e) B Coy 74th M.G.Bn during operations will be in Divisional Reserve and ready to move forward at short notice.
(f) The Machine Gun barrage will move 250 yards in front of the 18 pdr barrage and will lift 250 yards at a time.

E Buxton
Major,
Brigade Major,
230th Infantry Brigade.

Issued to Signals at

Same distribution.

SECRET.

Copy No....8

230th INFANTRY BRIGADE
BATTLE INSTRUCTIONS No 2.

16th August 1918.

In amplification of BATTLE INSTRUCTIONS No.1 issued yesterday.

1. The 1st Australian Bde, which is attacking on our right, will up to the 1st objective have the 4th Australian Battn on its left (O.C. Major Mackenzie). The 3rd Australian Battn will leap-frog on the 1st objective and continue the advance to the second and Exploitation objectives (C.O. Major Burrett).

2. Units will detail the following to establish touch at points mentioned:-
(a) THE SUFFOLKS.
i. 1 section on the right just in rear of 1st objective - sunk road L.4.a.8.4 - with 4th Australian Battn.
ii. 1 platoon on left 1st objective - sunk road F.28.d.2.0 - with Sussex.
iii. 1 section L.3.d.9.8 with 4th Australian Battn.
(b) THE BUFFS.
i. 1 section F.29.d.9.0 with 3rd Australian Battn.
ii. 1 platoon on right at 2nd objective A.25.d.2.0 with 3rd Aust.Bn.
iii. 1 platoon on left at 2nd objective F.30.c.1.9 with Somersets.
iv. 1 platoon on right Exploitation line A.26.d.5.0.
v. 1 platoon left Exploitation line A.26.d.5.9.
(c) THE SUSSEX.
i. 1 platoon on right 1st objective F.28.d.2.0 with Suffolks.
× ii. 1 platoon on left 1st objective F.28.b.3.4 TOINE POST with 231st Brigade.
(d) THE SOMERSETS.
i. 1 platoon on right 2nd objective F.30.c.1.9 with Buffs.
× ii. 1 platoon on left 2nd objective - BENJAMIN Trench F.29.b.8.9 - with 10th K.S.L.I.
iii. 1 platoon on right Exploitation line A.26.d.5.9.
iv. 1 platoon on left " " A.26.b.2.9.

3. Brigade Advance Report Centre and Visual Stations will open as the advance progresses about the following localities:-
(a) F.28.d.7.3.
(b) F.28.d.central.
There will also be a Divisional Visual Station at K.3.central. It will be connected by wire with Div.H.Q. and is for the use of all formations. The call will be "V.S".

4. POWER BUZZERS. Each attacking Brigade will be provided with two complete Loop-Sets, providing communication for 2 Battn H.Q, one Report Centre & one Bde H.Q. Messages can be sent in clear when fighting is in progress at the discretion of C.O's.

5. Pigeons are being supplied to Battalions.

[signature]
Major,
Brigade Major,
230th Infantry Brigade.

Issued to Signals at

Same distribution.

SECRET. Copy No.8..

230th INFANTRY BRIGADE

BATTLE INSTRUCTIONS No.I. 15th August 1918.

Ref.Map - Sheets 62c N.E. & 62b, 1/20,000.

1. (a) The 74th Division, in conjunction with 1st Australian Division on right and 58th Division on left, is about to attack and capture the enemy positions forward of the HINDENBURG Line.
(b) Of the 74th Divn, the 230th Inf.Bde on the right and 231st Inf.Bde on left, each reinforced by one Battalion 229th Bde, will deliver the assault.
(c) Of the 230th Inf.Bde, the Suffolks on the right and Sussex on left will lead the attack and capture the GREEN line.
(d) The Buffs on right and Somersets on left will follow the attack, subsequently passing through the Suffolks and Sussex respectively on the Green line and continue the advance to capture and consolidate RED line. Those two Battalions will be prepared subsequently to take advantage of any opportunity - should such favourable situation arise - to push on to the EXPLOITATION line.
(e) Details as to Battalions and Brigades on our flanks will be communicated later.

2. ZERO day and hour will be notified later.

3. (a) The boundaries of the attack for the 230th Inf.Bde are as follows:-
SOUTH boundary:- L.1.d.0.3 - L.2.d.0.3 - L.3.d.0.3 - F.29.c.0.0.
NORTH boundary:- E.29.cent - F.25.cent - F.27.a.9.1 - F.28.b.35.35 - F.29.b.90.85 - A.26.b.00.85.
Inter-BATTALION Boundary:- L.1.a.0.8 - L.3.b.10.8 - F.28.c.10.0 - F.29.c.cent - F.29.d.10.9 - thence due East.
(b) The start line is the present front line, but the Suffolks will start South of the COLOGNE River with right on Sunken Road L.8.a.2.7.
(c) Objective lines are as follows:-
1st objective, GREEN line = L.4.b.9.0 - L.4.b.4.6 - F.28.d.2.0 - CONNOR POST - Stone Post and continuation of trench system North.
2nd objective, RED line = A.25.d.3.0 - F.30.c.7.8 - F.30.c.3.7 - Rifleman Post - Benjamin Post, etc.
3. Line of EXPLOITATION = A.26.d.central - QUENNEMONT PIT LANE.

4. The attack will be carried out under a barrage supported by moving batteries and a machine gun barrage. Barrage maps will be issued in due course.
Heavy artillery will be engaging enemy batteries and other selected targets.

5. Each Battalion will have ½ section 'A' Coy M.G.Bn attached, and Buffs & Somersets will each also have 2 L.T.M's.

6. The Buffs will take over the portion of the front line now held by the Suffolks in L.1.a & c on X/Y night.

7. Further instructions will follow.

8. ACKNOWLEDGE.

Major,
Brigade Major,
230th Infantry Brigade.

Issued to Signals at

Copies to:-
1 10 Buffs
2 15 Suffolks
3 16 Sussex
4 12 Somerset L.I.
5 'A' Coy M.G.Bn.
6 L.T.M.B.
7 44 Bde R.F.A.
8 231 Inf.Bde.
9 2nd Australian Bde.

SECRET. 230th INFANTRY BRIGADE Copy No.8...
BATTLE INSTRUCTIONS No.4.

17th Septr 1918.

1. The 2 sections M.G.Battn attached to the Brigade will form up on the starting line, 1 section immediately in rear of each of the Suffolks & Sussex & in front of the Somersets (on the left) & will cooperate with the attacking Battns throughout assisting the advance to the 1st objective by covering fire. Carrying parties required will be obtained from the two leading Battns and these parties will remain with the Sections throughout when the latter are supporting the advance of the second line Battns to the 2nd and Exploitation objectives.
2. Attacking Battns will operate on a 2-Company frontage. When forming up on the starting line rear Companies must be closed up to clear the present front line trenches (required for rear Battns). As soon as the advance commences, rear Companies will shake out to about 1000 yards distance from the front lines.
During the interval between the time the barrage first comes down and the first lift, the leading line should gradually work forward to as near the barrage as compatible with safety. It is to be impressed upon all that the closer the leading line advances behind the barrage the less the danger of suffering casualties from enemy M.G's & rifle fire.
3. The Buffs & Somersets are, when they first move off from the present front trenches, to clear East of those trenches as quickly as possible and then subsequently to shake out into artillery formation. The one object is to get these Battalions clear of the probable enemy barrage line ere this fire is put down and thus insure that they will be able to move forward again in time to push on to attack the 2nd objective. Every advantage to be taken in the interim for obtaining cover from enemy fire. BUT in the event of the Suffolks or Sussex being unable to reach the 1st objective line without support from other infantry, such support will be given by the Buffs and Somersets respectively.
4. Mopping-up parties detailed from the Suffolks and Sussex for TEMPLEUX LE GUERARD and the Quarries will not leave those neighbourhoods till they have disposed of every enemy above and below ground. All cellars and dug-outs are to be guarded at once and kept under guard until this has been done. Mopping-up parties will then rejoin their Battalions in the Green line.
5. Any prisoners taken are to be utilised to carry back our wounded with a minimum escort composed where possible of our own walking wounded.

[signature]
Major,
Brigade Major,
230th Infantry Brigade.

Issued to Signals at

Same distribution.

SECRET.

Copy No.7..

230th INFANTRY BRIGADE ORDER No.69.

20 Septr 1918

1. (a) The 74th Divn is attacking tomorrow morning in a N.E direction, objective the Blue Line A.20.d.0.4 - A.20.a.0.2 - A.14.c.0.3 - A.14.a.1.0 - A.8.c.0.4. The 3rd Australian Bde on the right and 18th Divn on left are also attacking to a similar objective line South and North respectively.
South Divisional Boundary A.25.d.0.0 thence N.E to A.20.c.8.1.
(b) The attack of the 74th Divn is being carried out by the 230th Bde on right and 231st Bde on left, while the 229th Bde is to take over the defenceof the Green line.
Boundary between attacking Brigades - Cross Roads F.29.b.8.8 (inclusive to 230th Bde) thence in a N.E direction to A.14.c.1.3.
2. The attack of the Bde will be carried out by Buffs on right and Sussex on left, each on a 2-Company front. Boundary between Battalions F.30.a.0.1 - A.20.c.0.7.
The Suffolks will be in support and will be disposed by Zero hour - two Companies in the area VALLEY POST - RIFLEMAN POST - Post Cross Roads F.29.b.8.8 and system trenches F.29.b - two Companies and Battalion H.Q. TEMPLEUX SWITCH and TOINE POST.
3. The attacking Battalions will advance behind a creeping barrage lifting 100 yards each 4 minutes. There will probably be a pause of half an hour on line parallel to and 200 yards N.E of WIGAN WAY A.19.d.10.5 - A.19.b.0.8 to enable 231st Bde to 'leap-frog' its attacking Companies. During this pause Buffs will where possible proceed with consolidation of Blue Line. Further advance of Sussex will continue when barrage again goes forward.
4. (a) The forming-up and barrage lines are not yet definitely fixed. As soon as known they and also the barrage table will be communicated. The forming-up line will probably be ZOGDA Trench in F.30.d and sunken road F.30.b.4.0 - F.29.b.8.8 with the barrage starting line about 200 yards in advance.
By Zero minus ½ hour the Buffs and Sussex will have their leading Companies deployed on this line and support Companies close behind so that the whole (less reserve Company in case of Buffs) may advance when the barrage commences to move forward.
(b) One section M.Gs will accompany each of the attacking Battalions to support advance and assist in consolidation of objective line. On attaining this line Buffs and Sussex will be disposed in depth - each retaining his Companies for defence of front system - main strength at QUINNEMONT FARM and TOP TRENCH SPUR respectively.
REAR DEFENCES.
BUFFS 1 Coy trench system A.25.b central
1 Coy F.30.c.6.3 post area.
SUSSEX 1 Coy QUENNET COPSE and QUENNET HIGH TRENCH
1 Coy QUENNET LOW TRENCH and Battn H.Q ARTAXERXES POST.
(c) 1 section M.Gs will be disposed on these same rear lines and the remaining section along the front held by the Suffolks as soon as the situation admits of these positions being taken up.
5. The Buffs and Sussex will each detail necessary carrying parties for their attached M.G sections and the Suffolks will detail the parties required for M.Gs as in 4 (c).
6. Attacking Battalions will establish the usual platoon liaison posts for touch on both flanks as soon as the objective line is reached.
7. An Advanced Report Centre, visualise and telephone, will open before Zero hour in Artaxerxes Post about F.29.b.0.4.
8. PRISONERS OF WAR. The P/W Cage will be situated at E.27.d.8.8. A screen of M.M.P will be placed along the main RONSSOY - HARGICOURT Road from F.15 central, F.15.d.7.8, F.21.c.4.8 to L.5.c.2.5, covering the Divisional Front. Escorts must be warned that they are only to hand over Prisoners to representatives 74th Division. Where possible they should be instructed to take them via Brigade H.Q. where they will be passed on to the P/W Cage.
9. DUMPS. A dump of S.A.A, Grenades, Fireworks and Reserve Water has been established at F.28.a.4.2 from which Units should refill.
10. Zero hour will probably be 5 a.m.
11. Brigade H.Q. remain at present position.
12. ACKNOWLEDGE.

[signature]
Major
Brigade Major,
230th Infantry Brigade.

P.T.O.

Issued to Signals at

Copies to:-
1 Buffs
2 Suffolks
3 Sussex
4 'A' Coy M.G.Bn
5 L.T.M.B.
6 74th Divn
7 231st Inf.Bde
8 2nd Australian Bde
9 44th Bde R.F.A.

SECRET.   Copy No. 10

ADDENDA No, 2. to Brigade Order No,71.

Reference Map 1,20,000. Sheets 36a and 36.

1. Relief of 58th Brigade by 230th Infantry Brigade will be carried out as follows:-

10th Buffs	9th R.W.F.	Right Battalion.
16th Sussex	9th W.R.	Left "
15th Suffolks	2nd Wilts	Support.
230th L.T.M.B.	58th L.T.M.B.	H.Q. by Support Brigade H.Q.

2. 15th Suffolks will carry out relief by day. They will entrain at 12.30 p.m. and 2 Coys will detrain at EMPEROR Siding, if possible, X.10 c 52 55.

Two Coys and Bn. H.Q. at LE TOURET.

Part of B.H.Q. will entrain with 15th Suffolks.

3. Trains for remainder of Brigade will leave CHOCQUES Station at 3.30 p.m.

Units will march independently to entraining Point. 10th Buffs will entrain at 3.30 p.m., 16th Sussex at 3.45 p.m., B.H.Q. and B.H.F.P at 4 p.m.

L.T.M.B. will entrain with those Battalions in whose lines their guns are.

Lt. H.F.Wood, 15th Suffolks, will be entraining Officer for Brigade and will be at CHOCQUES STATION by 12 noon.

4. Details of relief to be made by C,Os. concerned.

5. All Defence Orders, photographs, trench maps, trench and area stores will be taken over.

Battn. will also take over all arrangements for working parties required for work in Line of Retention.

6. Relief complete to be wired to B.H.Q. at LOISNE CHATEAU, X 28 a. using code word "NOT REQUIRED".

7. B.H.Q. will close in present position and reopen at LOISNE CHATEAU at 1 p.m.

8. Command of Sector will pass on completion of relief.

9. ACKNOWLEDGE.

[signature]
Major.
Bde.Major.
230th Inf.Bde.

File

Issued at.

Copies to:

10th Buffs.
15th Suffolks
16th Sussex
230th L.T.M.B.
Bde. Signal Officer.
B.H.F.P.
58th Brigade.
74th Division.
File.

SECRET.

ADDENDUM NO. 1
, to -
230th INFANTRY BRIGADE ORDER No. 71.

29th Septr 1918.

The 230th Infantry Brigade Group will entrain at CHOCQUES D.5.b.3.4 on the Light Railway at 3.30 p.m. on 1st October. They will detrain at LE TOURET X.16.c.8.8, where they will be met by their Cookers and Lewis Gun transport.
15th Suffolks will precede the remainder of the Group and will entrain at 12.30 p.m. This Battalion will carry out relief by daylight.
Remainder of the transport will proceed at the same time as the Cookers and Lewis Gun limbers but will be met by guides at detraining station under Battalion arrangements and will be taken immediately to their new positions.
15th Suffolks are expected to arrive at detraining station at 2.30 p.m. and the remainder at 5.30 p.m.

L Buxton
Major,
Brigade Major,
230th Infantry Brigade.

Distribution same as for
Bde Order No.71.

SECRET.   Copy No. 5

230th INFANTRY BRIGADE ORDER No. 71.

1. The 74th Division will relieve 19th Division in the line. 230th Inf.Bde will relieve the Right Brigade in the line on the night October 1st/2nd. 10th Buffs will be the right front Battalion and 16th Sussex the left front Battalion. 15th Suffolks in reserve.

2. The Brigade will march to CHOCQUES on October 1st and will travel on from thence by Light Railway.

3. Advance parties as below will travel by lorries on September 30th:-

Battalions.	L.T.M.B.
C.O. & Adjutant.	C.O.
Company Commanders.	
1 Offr & N.C.O. per platoon.	
Intelligence Officer.	
Signal Officer.	

These Officers less the Battalion Commander will await the arrival of Battalions in the line.

4. C.O's will arrange for Cookers to meet troops at ~~CHOCQUES Station~~ rail head on Oct. 1st to give the men hot food prior to going into the line.

5. Transport will move by road. Distances will be kept in accordance with Divisional March Standing Orders.

6. Lorries for the Advance Parties will be at Brigade H.Q. at 8 a.m. Rations for October 1st will be taken.

7. Further orders will be issued later.

[signature]

Major,
Brigade Major,
230th Infantry Brigade.

29th September 1918.

Copies to:-

No. 1 10th Buffs
2 15th Suffolks
3 16th Sussex
4 ~~xxxxxxx~~ L.T.M.B.
5 File.
6 449 Coy A.S.C.
7 R.M.RE
8 FLD Amb.
9 DIV

Vol. 7.

Headquarters,
230th Inf. Bde.
(74th Division)

October 1918.

169th Inf Bde

Jan 1918.

Volume No. ______

BRITISH SALONIKA FORCE

WAR DIARY.

26th Division

Vol. No.	Unit	PERIOD From	To
31.	C. R. E.	1. 5. 18.	31. 5. 18.
29.	107th Field Co. R. E.	1. 5. 18.	31. 5. 18.
30	108th Field Co. R. E.	1. 5. 18.	31. 5. 18.
30	131st. Field Co. R. E.	1. 5. 18.	31. 5. 18.
31.	Divisional Signal ~~School~~ Coy	1. 5. 18.	31. 5. 18.

A.P. & S.D., Alex./No. 752/8:5:17/3000 (50041G/53) W. M. & Co.

1 | 230 Inf Bde | HQ Qrs 230th Inf Bde

Instructions regarding War Diaries and Intelligence Summaries are contained in F. S. Regs., Part II. and the Staff Manual respectively. Title pages will be prepared in manuscript.

BEF

WAR DIARY
~~or~~
~~INTELLIGENCE SUMMARY.~~
(Erase heading not required.)

Oct. 1918

Army Form C. 2118.

Oct 18

Ref map 1:20000 36 SW

Vol 7

Place	Date	Hour	Summary of Events and Information	Remarks and references to Appendices
ALLOUAGNE	1		Bde moved up in the line by light Rly from CHOQUES to LE TOURET relieving 59th Div – 10 Buffs went in the line on the right, relieving 9 R[illegible], 16 Sussex on the left relieving 9 W.R., 15 Suffolks in support relieving 2 Wilts – BHQ opened at LOISNE CHATEAU at 1pm.	
	2.	0445	Relief not complete till 0445 –	
		1100	[illegible] leaving enemy vacated line in front. Front line [illegible]	
		1600	This reported past road in S18 going East with objective LA BASSEE – AUBERS ~~[illegible]~~ FROMELLES line of trenches, & asked them to push on patrols and follow on.	
			Communication was bad –	
			10 Buffs unable to reach objective owing to darkness – line reached T13b15.90 – T19a6.7. 16 Sussex covering HALPEGARBE –	
			Roads reported mined (booby traps) and wired, impassable for [illegible]	
		2200	Bde start ordered for 0630 tomorrow to first objective, thence patrols to go forward as before –	
			Right and left Bdes ahead of us. 231 Bde took over from Bde on our left –	
	3.	0630	Advance to AUBERS – FROMELLES LINE and [illegible] line covering HERLIES with right refused to cover GRAVELIN	
		1700	[illegible] of Bn reports, [illegible] forward to 10 Buffs HQ to take forward [illegible] good ground forward if enemy continues to retire.	

[illegible] Capt
Bde Maj 230 Inf Bde

D. D. & L., London, E.C.
(A3004) Wt. W1771/M2-31 750,000 5/17 Sch. 52 Forms/C2118/14

2

230 Inf Bde

BEF

Instructions regarding War Diaries and Intelligence Summaries are contained in F.S. Regs., Part II. and the Staff Manual sespectively. Title pages will be prepared in manuscript.

WAR DIARY
or
INTELLIGENCE SUMMARY.
(Erase heading not required).

Oct 1918

Army Form C. 2118.

Place	Date	Hour	Summary of Events and Information	Remarks and references to Appendices.
S10 x	3.	0800	Bde HQ moved to S10.a, and later at 1000 to HALPEGARBE.	Ref map 1/20000 36 S.W.
		1330.	10th Buffs had reached 2nd objective - SUGAR FACTORY - WICRES - LE WAQUET. The Sussex had reached East of HERLIES by 1630 and E. of WICRES by 1535 with 231 Inf Bde now left in FOURNES	
		1710	Buffs on No 5 line East of GRAND and BASSE RUE. Sussex to left rear of Buffs facing E.N.E. with their left in S.W. outskirts of FOURNES. 231 Inf Bde continued the line through FOURNES.	
		1500.	Bde HQ moved to huts in HERLIES.	
			Cable shortage [illegible] of the [illegible]	
		1740	Division ordered no forward move ~~again~~ today. Line at present BASSE RUE, FOURNES, PETITE HAUBOURDIN for the right. Bde on right had not kept up and was ~~on the line~~ W. of line LE MARAIS HOCRON - SAINGHIN.	
	4.	0800	15 Suffolks went through leading Bns and the advance was resumed on a one Bn front to first objective, line U22b cent - WAVRIN - Northwards along line E of Rly to O29b+d.) The Buffs carried on in this advance and 16 Sussex in Reserve	

J. Buxton Major
230 Inf Bde

A.P. & S.D., Alex./2009/50025A/11 : 17/5M. W.M. & Co.

3.

230 Inf Bde

B.E.F.

Oct 1918

Instructions regarding War Diaries and Intelligence Summaries are contained in F.S. Regs., Part. II. and the Staff Manual sespectively. Title pages will be prepared in manuscript.

WAR DIARY
or
INTELLIGENCE SUMMARY.
(Erase heading not required).

Army Form C. 2118.

Place	Date	Hour	Summary of Events and Information	Remarks and references to Appendices.
HERLIES	4	0910	15 Suffolks reached first objective in touch with KSLI on the left.	
		1030	Advance towards second objective Canal Bank with bridgehead LA PLANCHE DES SANTES	
		1100	Owing to situation on the right 15 Suffolks failed to advance - Enemy MG. from DON neighbourhood. Batten on right in U22a.	1:20000 Map 36 SW
		1420	Ordered to push forward to test the Canal Defences. 10 Buffs ordered to look after the right flank.	
			The 231 Bde were not quite up to us owing to their left having met with considerable opposition.	
			GOC and BGGS Corps visited Bde HQ during the morning.	
			Patrols found a strong bridgehead held by the enemy with a lot of M.Gs west of the Canal. Bde took up a defensive position covering LATTRES & WAVRIN - 10 Buffs in Support - 16 Sussex in Reserve. The Buffs had to post one Coy in the line on the right of 15 Suffolks linking up with 166 Bde.	
	5		Our patrols every where met by M.G. fire. Which appears to be [illegible]	
		~~1400~~	~~Cross Roads at HERLIES blown up, crater 35 feet by 15 [illegible] no casualties~~	

A.P. & S.D., Alex./2009/50025A/11 : 17/5M. W.M. & Co.

[illegible] Bn
230 [illegible]

4/ 230 Inf Bde

Instructions regarding War Diaries and Intelligence Summaries are contained in F.S. Regs., Part. II. and the Staff Manual sespectively. Title pages will be prepared in manuscript.

BEF

WAR DIARY
or
INTELLIGENCE SUMMARY.
(Erase heading not required).

Oct 1918

Army Form C. 2118.

Place	Date	Hour	Summary of Events and Information	Remarks and references to Appendices.
	5	1200	GOC + all Brigadiers conferred at HQ 230 Brigade on the situation.	Ref Sheet 36 1/40000
		1700	Cross Roads at HERLIES went up, crater 35 feet by 15' deep. No casualties	
	6	1500	Brigade Head Quarters closed at HERLIES and opened at WICRES	
	7	0000 to 0830	Patrols found COULIN and parts of BEUSIGNIES clear, one patrol reaching Canal S of WAVRIN. Later patrols were unable to reach these places owing to M G and artillery fire. Enemy reported digging in immediately E of BEUSIGNIES	
		1500	GOC Div, BGC 231 + BGC 166 visited Brigade H Qrs during the afternoon. Brigade Major sited a defensive line	
			During the night Battalion Relief. 10th Buffs relieved 15th Suffolks in the line and extended their flank northwards owing to widening of Divisional Front. 16th Sussex took over the outpost line of resistance from the 10th Buffs and 15th Suffolks went into Brigade Reserve S of FOURNES.	
	8	0430	Battalion Relief completed.	
			During the night 10th Buffs sent out 9 Patrols who found the enemy occupying ground between themselves + the Canal.	
	9	0900	Brigade received orders to reconnoitre the Right Sector of the 231st Brigade Front with a view to sidestepping about 1000 yards northwards and handing over the greater portion of the 230th Brigade Front to the 166th Brigade who were on the right.	

D C Gidney Capt BM
230th Inf Bde

A.P. & S.D., Alex./2009/50025A/11: 17/5M. W.M. & Co.

5/

230 Inf Bde

Instructions regarding War Diaries and Intelligence Summaries are contained in F.S. Regs., Part. II. and the Staff Manual sespectively. Title pages will be prepared in manuscript.

BEF

WAR DIARY
or
INTELLIGENCE SUMMARY.
(Erase heading not required).

Oct 1918

Army Form C. 2118.

Place	Date	Hour	Summary of Events and Information	Remarks and references to Appendices.
	9		Temporary Major J.B. DODGE arrived and assumed command of the 15 Suffolks. The Division stated that as soon as another Battalion became vacant Major DODGE would get it and hand over the command of the 15th Suffolks to Major GRISSELL.	
		1000	B.G.C conferred with BGC 229th Inf Bde re Battle Line and Outpost line of resistance	
		1400	BGC conferred with BGC 166th Inf Bde on the same subjects	
	10		GOC Div ~~took~~ BGC to confer with GOC 55th Division on Corps Battle Line	
			Brigade sideslipped northwards. 16 Sussex relieved 10th KSLI in the line and part of the 10th Buffs. 10th Buffs relieved by 166th Bde	
	11		Army Commander visited BHQ.	
	12		Major J.B. DODGE took over command of 16th Sussex vice Lt Col EDWARDS	
			Conference at BHQ re Scheme.	
	13		Battalion Relief. 15th Suffolks relieved 16th Sussex in the line, ~~when~~ the latter going into reserve. 10th Buffs came into support	
		2345	Relief completed. The line was slightly advanced during the night to obtain touch on the right flank	
			D C Godwy Capt BM 230th Inf Bde	

A.P. & S.D., Alex./$\frac{2009}{50025A}$/11 : 17/5M. W.M. & Co.

6

230 Inf Bde

WAR DIARY
or
INTELLIGENCE SUMMARY.
(Erase heading not required).

Oct 1918

Army Form C. 2118.

Instructions regarding War Diaries and Intelligence Summaries are contained in F.S. Regs., Part. II. and the Staff Manual sespectively. Title pages will be prepared in manuscript.

BEF

Place	Date	Hour	Summary of Events and Information	Remarks and references to Appendices.
	14		GOC sent a letter to 15th Suffolks congratulating them on their excellent patrolling on October 9th.	Ref Sheet 36 1/40000
		1100	15th Suffolks moved forward to line LACHERIE – O 36 central (S of SANTES) with patrols in front. Brigade on right had not yet moved	
		1120	Coys moved up to road in O 36 a + d (S of SANTES). OP established LACHERIE	
	15		Advance began. Local Mn Gn opposition. Both flanks refused which prevented the Brigade getting to the Canal. Bde H Qrs moved to La VALLEE Chateau (U 4 c Sheet 36 SW 1/20000), 15th Suffolks to La HAIE, 10th Buffs to QUINQUIBUS, 16th Sussex to E end of FOURNES. Division to FOURNES Chateau.	
	16.		Repeated attempts to reach canal frustrated by Mn G fire, altho' the Bde on our right succeeded in crossing + took [illegible] BAC de HAVRIN.	
			BHQ move to CARNOYE Farm (O 33 a) E of FOURNES	
	17	0430	Enemy vanished during the night altho' they were firing heavily with Mn Gs from the Canal as late as 0430. Guns however had not been firing for several hours. Enemy reported by civilians to have Evacuated LILLE. Bde was not in touch all day. Objectives (i) Canal (ii) Road N + S through EMMERIN	

D C Gilroy Capt BM
230th Inf Bde

A.P. & S.D., Alex./2009/50025A/11 : 17/5M. W.M. & Co.

1/ 230th Inf Bde BEF

Instructions regarding War Diaries and Intelligence Summaries are contained in F.S. Regs., Part. II. and the Staff Manual sespectively. Title pages will be prepared in manuscript.

WAR DIARY
or
INTELLIGENCE SUMMARY.
(Erase heading not required).

Oct 1918

Army Form C. 2118.

Place	Date	Hour	Summary of Events and Information	Remarks and references to Appendices.
	17		(iii) WATTIGNIES, L'ARBRISSEAU, LOOS. These were reached during the afternoon by the 15th Suffolks. The 10th Buffs were then pushed through to gain the Railway Line through MERCHIN, which was not accomplished and a line was taken up E of FACHES.	Ref Sheet 36 1/40000
		2100	10th Buffs were relieved E of FACHES by (one Battn of the) 231st Infantry Brigade.	
		2300	15th Suffolks were withdrawn from the L'ARBRISSEAU line when the 231st Infantry Brigade had passed through.	
		2330	BHQ established L'ARBRISSEAU. 10th Buffs billeted WATTIGNIES. 15th Suffolks + LTMB L'ARBRISSEAU. 16th Sussex FLEQUIERES. Major I. BUXTON, BM 230th Inf Bde left for Junior Staff Course CAMBRIDGE Capt H. S. SHARP, F+F Yeomanry officiated	
	18	1130	Orders to move to LESQUIN – RONCHIN area	
		1500	BHQ established LESQUIN (W6a 8.9). Captain D.C GILROY, 3rd Hussars arrived + took over the duties of Brigade major. [redacted] KG	
		1830	Battalions billeted as follows 16th Sussex, 15th Suffolks + LTMB in RONCHIN 10th Buffs LESQUIN. 179 AFA Bde attached to 230th Inf Bde and billeted in LESQUIN.	
		2130	Orders to reconnoitre a main line of resistance with a view to a move.	

D C Gilroy Capt B M
230th Inf Bde

A.P. & S.D., Alex./2009/50025A/II: 17/5M. W.M. & Co.

8/

230 Inf Bde

Instructions regarding War Diaries and Intelligence Summaries are contained in F.S. Regs., Part. II. and the Staff Manual sespectively. Title pages will be prepared in manuscript.

BEF

WAR DIARY
or
INTELLIGENCE SUMMARY.
(Erase heading not required).

Oct 1918

Army Form C. 2118.

Place	Date	Hour	Summary of Events and Information	Remarks and references to Appendices.
	19	0800	BGC, BM + Battn Comdrs reconnoitre two main lines of resistance (I) FORT SAINGHIN, SAINGHIN, ASCQ and (II) FORT SAINGHIN, SAINGHIN BATTERIE du CAMP FRANCAIS, the former being the best.	Ref Sheets 36 37 1/40000
		1230	GOC Div + BG KENNEDY visited BHQ.	
		1700	BHQ closed LESQUIN + Brigade moved to SAINGHIN, CHERENG, GRUSON, AUSTAING and TRESSIN.	
		1950	BHQ established CHERENG (m 21 a 6.1). Billets 10^E Buffs SAINGHIN, CHERENG. 15^E Suffolks 16^E Sussex, LTMB CHERENG. D Coy M G ~~Bn~~ AUSTAING. 179 AFA Bde GRUSON.	
		2300	one section No 5 Field Coy RARE attached to Brigade + billeted CHERENG	
		2359	Orders to move 0800 20^E to BAISIEUX - CAMPHIN area.	
	20	0830	BHQ closed CHERENG.	
		1040	BHQ opened BAISIEUX (N19 a 5.8). ~~LTMB~~ Billeted at BAISIEUX, LTMB N19a, RE Sect N19a, 15^E Suffolks N19c, 10^E Buffs N19c. 16^E Sussex, D Coy MG and 179 Bde AFA at CAMPHIN.	
		1200	GOC Div + BG KENNEDY visited BHQ	
		1740	Verbal message by telephone GSO1 that Bde stands fast tonight	

DC Gilroy Capt BM
230^E Inf Bde

A.P. & S.D., Alex./2009/50025A/11 : 17/5M. W.M. & Co.

9/ 230 Inf Bde

Instructions regarding War Diaries and Intelligence Summaries are contained in F.S. Regs., Part. II. and the Staff Manual sespectively. Title pages will be prepared in manuscript.

BEF

WAR DIARY
or
INTELLIGENCE SUMMARY.
(Erase heading not required).

Oct 1918

Army Form C. 2118.

Place	Date	Hour	Summary of Events and Information	Remarks and references to Appendices.
	21	0800	Outpost line of resistance reconnoitred E of LAMAIN and HERTAING. Dispositions made by 10th Buffs and 16th Sussex.	Ref Sheet 37 1/40000
		0845	German ammunition dump blew up in a house in BAISIEUX occupied by 2 Coys of 15th Suffolks. 3 men missing, believed burnt to death, 5 wounded. A foot inspection was taking place at the time, to be followed by a Kit Inspection. All equipment was lost	
		1200	Brig Gen KENNEDY visited BHQ & conferred with the Acting Brigadier.	
		1530	One officer + a weak platoon of the 15th Suffolks ordered to picket SIN RE dumps to prevent looting by the civilians	
		1730	GOC Division telephoned complaining of slackness of Bde in saluting etc. Act Brigadier wrote a strong memo to all units.	
	22	1830	Orders received by telephone for 230 Bde to relieve 229 Bde in Line. Warned all units	
		2130	Detailed orders (D.O No 106) for above arrived. Issued more detailed orders to units	
	23	1030	BGC + BM liaised with 229th Bde regarding relief. Got all dispositions	
		1200	Div Order No 106 cancelled by telephone	
		1500	Div Order No 106 to come into force night 24/25. Informed all units	
	24	1000	Issued ~~OO~~ 230 Inf Bde OO No 79. Detailed orders for Relief	
		1030	Act BGC + BM reconnoitred a Main Outpost line of resistance. Scheme forwarded to Div	
		2240	Relief completed. A few casualties from shells, all slight. 10th Buffs 1 off 5 OR. 16th Sussex 1 off 1 OR. 15th Suffolks 2 OR	
	25	0430	Quiet night. Patrols unable to move about on account of MG Fire.	
			During the morning Act BGC liaised with 164th Inf Bde on right and arranged Defence Scheme	
			Staff Captain visited 15th Suffolks, 16th Sussex, Rear HQrs 10th Buffs + all transport lines	
		1400	Defence Scheme sent to Div Hd Qrs	

D C Gilroy Capt BM
230th Inf Bde

A.P. & S.D., Alex./2009/50025A/11 : 17/5M. W.M. & Co.

10/

230 Inf Bde

BEF

WAR DIARY
or
INTELLIGENCE SUMMARY.
(Erase heading not required.)

Oct 1918

Army Form C. 2118.

Instructions regarding War Diaries and Intelligence Summaries are contained in F. S. Regs., Part II. and the Staff Manual respectively. Title pages will be prepared in manuscript.

Place	Date	Hour	Summary of Events and Information	Remarks and references to Appendices
	25		During the afternoon Brigade Major liaised with 172 Inf Bde on left re Defence Scheme	Ref Sheet 37 1/40000
		1500	The troop King Edward's Horse transferred to HQ 55th Division	
		1615 to 1715	10th Buffs heavily shelled with 4.2" and 5.9". Direct hit on Bde O.P at O 26 b 2.3. Casualties slight 1 Killed 7 wounded. Some gas was fired.	
		2100	Provisional Orders for a forward move ~~[illegible]~~ issued	
	26	0400	Quiet night. Situation normal. No weakening of enemy. Patrols unable to move owing to M. Gs	
			During morning Act B G C visited 10th Buffs, 15th Suffolks, 16th Sussex. In the afternoon Bde Major inspected trenches dug in main outpost line of defence.	
		1715	Intermittent shelling + M G bursts all day on 10th Buffs & T M shelling. Difficult to locate	
	27	0400	Quiet night. Enemy M.G. still active against our patrols. ORCQ received attention from shells.	
			During the morning the Bde Major inspected trenches dug in Outpost Line of Resistance, afterwards visiting Battn Hd Qrs of 15th Suffolks + 16th Sussex. In the afternoon the act BGC visited 10th Buffs.	
		1500	Air reported British Troops + Transport entering TOURNAI. A patrol was sent out to ascertain the accuracy of this statement ~~which was~~ and was heavily fired on by M Gs, forcing withdrawal.	
		1630	10th Buffs shelled + Gassed.	
		1925	44th RFA Bde reported indications of a hostile withdrawal.	
		2000	Report that Gas (Mustard) in MARQUAIN this afternoon damaged Mules + Chargers of 16th Sussex 4 mules + 2 Chargers killed + several badly gassed.	
		2030	Issued new orders (B O O No 82) referring to Forward move, which cancelled B.O.O. No 80.	
	28	0335	Some shelling + gas on ORCQ. 10th Buffs report no signs of enemy withdrawal	
		0945	G O C Div visited B H Q + took acting B G C to inspect Outpost Line of Resistance	
		1100	Issued orders for ~~the~~ Inter Battalion relief night of 28/29 inst. B O O No 81. Disposition changed by G O C's orders. Two Battalions to hold Outpost + Outpost Line of Resistance in depth. One Battalion in Bde Reserve in MARQUAIN	
		1700	Defence Scheme issued	
		2130	Battalion Relief completed	

D C Gilroy Capt B M
230th Inf Bde.

D. D. & L., London, E.C.
(10346) Wt W5300/P713 750,000 3/18 E 2688 Forms C/2118/16.

11

230 Inf Bde — BEF

WAR DIARY
or
INTELLIGENCE SUMMARY.
(Erase heading not required.)

Oct 1918

Army Form C. 2118.

Instructions regarding War Diaries and Intelligence Summaries are contained in F. S. Regs., Part II. and the Staff Manual respectively. Title pages will be prepared in manuscript.

Place	Date	Hour	Summary of Events and Information	Remarks and references to Appendices
	29	0100 - 0200	Heavy shelling of MARQUAIN by HE and Gas	
		1100	Issued 230 Inf Bde Order No 83. Relief of 230 Inf Bde by 231 Inf Bde night of 30/31 Oct	Ref Sheet 37 1/40000
		1230	Army Commander + GOC Div visited BHQ	
		1600	Brigadier General A A KENNEDY CMG refused [illegible] from Division.	
	30	0230 - 0430	Considerable activity on front line by M.G. T.M.S and 77mm Guns.	
		1200	Lt Col Spence Jones left to act as BGC 231 Inf Bde	
		1500	Battalion Commanders conference at BHQ re Occupying TOURNAI after an enemy withdrawal	
		1600	Shelling on Left Sector subnormal. Normal on Right Sector	
		1800	Issued Special Instruction by TOURNAI (230th) Brigade for the Occupation of TOURNAI	
		2220	Relief complete. Owing to breaking of wires, report late in arriving. Relief was completed 2100.	
			10th Buffs Billeted HERTAIN, 15th Suffolks HAUDION, 16th Sussex LAMAIN.	
	31	1800	Issued 230th Inf Bde Order NO 84 relative to holding main line of Resistance	

D C Gilroy Capt
BM. 230th Inf Bde

D. D. & L., London, E.C.
(10340) Wt W5300/P713 750,000 5/18 E 2688 Forms C/2118/15.

SECRET.

Brigade Order No 72.

---

1. After arrival at AUBERS LINE Patrols should be pushed out at dawn with view of establishing themselves along road running N and S through HERLIES (T.4.d.) to LA MALADERIE (T.11.c.1.1.) thence S.W. to GRAVELIN (T.21.b.2.b.) This Line will be occupied as soon as possible.

2. O.C. Bns. must furnish situation reports every 2 hours.

3. Patrol Leaders must show more enterprise. Once the objective is given cumbersome orders only complicate the task and delay operations.

4. Explain to all ranks that it is not usual for 74th Division to take a back seat in the hunt after the Bosche as has been the case to-day.

Major.
Bde.Major.
230th Inf.Bde.

2nd. Oct. 1918.

Cipies to.

O,C, 10th Buffs.
15th Suffolks.
16th R.Sussex.
19th Div.
87 Bde R.F.A.
166th Bde.
56th Bde.
File.

SECRET. Copy No......

230TH INFANTRY BRIGADE ORDER No.73.

Ref.Map:-36.S.W. 1:20,000. 6th October 1918.

1. On night of 7th/8th October 10th Buffs will relieve 15th Suffolks in the front line. The 16th Sussex will occupy the Line of Retention and 15th Suffolks will come into Reserve in position at present occupied by 16th Sussex.
Battalion Headquarters need not be changed.

2. All work in process will be handed over so as to ensure continuity.

3. The Battalion in Reserve will always supply the guard on Brigade Headquarters. This guard will be relieved daily at 1630, and and will be always mounted by an Officer. The Battalion Orderly Officer will be responsible for daily inspection of this guard.

4. Details of the relief will be arranged between C.O's concerned.

5. Trench Stores are in Line of Retention will be handed over.

[illegible]. Completion of reliefs will be wired to Brigade Headquarters by following code words:-

10th Buffs.	"NOTED".
15th Suffolks.	"WIRE PICKETS".
16th Sussex.	"YESPLEASE".

6. ACKNOWLEDGE.

Major,
Brigade Major.
230th Infantry Brigade.

Issued at. 2.00

Copies to:- No.1. 10th Buffs. No.5. 231st Inf.Bde.
2. 15th Suffolks. 6. 166th Inf.Bde.
3. 16th Sussex. 7. File.
4. 74th Division.

File

Copy No.....10.....

SECRET.

230th Infantry Brigade Order No. 74.

Ref. Map 1,20000. 36 S.W. and 36 S.E.

1. The Divisional and Brigade Boundaries are being readjusted as follows:-

South Divisional Boundary.
grid line between T.11. and T.17. (cross roads at T.11.c. inclusive to 55th Division) - T.12.c.0.0. - U.3.c.0.0. - grid line East between U.3. and U.9.

North Divisional Boundary.
O.20.c.0.0. - P.11.a.6.3.
P.11.b.8.3. - P.12.d.5.0. - Q.14.c.0.8. - thence eastward.

Inter Brigade Boundary.
O.31.d.2.4. - O.34.b.9.4. (Road junction inclusive to Right Brigade)
P.27.a.0.0. - thence eastward.

2. On night 10/11th Oct. the following reliefs will take place:-

(a). 230th Infantry Brigade will be relieved in the line as far north as the new southern Divisional boundary by 55th Div.

(b). 230th Inf.Brigade will relieve 231st Inf.Brigade ~~from new~~ ~~Inter Brigade Boundary~~ as far north as inter Brigade Boundary.

3. Above relief will be carried out as follows:-

(a). 16th Sussex will relieve 10th Buffs and 10th K.S.L.I. in the new Brigade front Line - from U.6.c.0.0. to O.34.b.9.4. O.C. 16th Sussex will to-morrow ascertain from Os.C. 10th K.S.L.I. and 10th Buffs exactly how this part of the line is at present held.

(b). 15th Suffolks will relieve 16th Sussex in the Outpost Line of Resistance.

(c). 10th Buffs on relief will come into Brigade Reserve.
Locations for all Units other than front line Battalions will be notified later.

4. The Corps battle line on completion of this readjustment will be the line MARQUILLIES - East of WICRES - East of FOURNES - BAS FLANDRE.

5. Details of reliefs will be arranged between C.Os. concerned.

6. The reconnaissances necessary for this readjustment will be carried out forthwith as far as possible.

7. Orders re L.T.M.B. will be issued to-morrow.

8. Sketch maps showing disposition of troops after the move will be submitted to B.H.Q. by 1800 on the 11th Oct.

9. Completion of relief will be wired to B.H.Q. by code words as follows:-

10th Buffs	MAPS.	16th Sussex	TRACING.
15th Suffolks	SKETCH.	230th L.T.M.B.	DRAWING.

10. ACKNOWLEDGE.

[signature]
Major.
Bde.Major.
230th INF.BDE.

8th Oct.,1918.

Copies to:-

10th Buffs. 1	231st INF.BDE. 6
15th Suffolks. 2	166th Inf.Bde. 7
16th Sussex. 3	87th Bde. R.F.A. 8
230th L.T.M. 4	74th M.G.Bn. 9
74th Division. 5	File. 10.

SECRET.   Copy No....6....

Addenda No. 1. to Brigade Order No, 74.

The Defence of the Southern half of the new Divisional Sector will be organised as follows:-

1. (a). Outpost Line held by A Battn. from grid line dividing squares U.5. and U.11. about U.5.d.6.0. to approx 0.34.b.9.4.

(b). Outpost Line of Resistance held by B.Battn. from U.8.b.5.8. to 0.33.c.7.9.

(c). Corps battle line,0.32.c.3.3. to U.2.a.3.6., thence South along Railway Embankment to U.2.c.7.7. U.1.d.9.5. to U.7.b.5.3. - (South of this Point in 55th Division area the line should proceed due South for500 yards following the form line) to be manned when necessary by C.Battn. from billets in wood about U.7.a.8.8.

This Battalion may in emergency be called upon to reinforce or counter attack to retake the Outpost Line of Resistance.

2. After the relief to-morrow night 10/11th

A Battn. will be 16th Sussex.
B. " " " 15th Suffolks.
C. " " " 10th Buffs.

3. B.Battn. will start after relief digging the Outpost Line of Resistance, placing Coys approx. as follows:-

(1). about U.8.b.5.9. to U.2.d.8.6.
(2). U.2.d.9.8. to U.2.b.9.6.
(3). U.3.b.0.9. to U.33.c.9.7.
(4). Support Coy. in a position to be chosen by O.C. 15th Suffolks.

This Battalion will find one platoon from No.1. Coy. to cover M.Gs. posted in Eastern edge of LA VALLEE Wood.

4. Every effort will be made to dig posts securely in at once and as far as possible every post should have an alternative position which will be utilised to fox the enemy.

The necessity for the greatest vigilance to be exercised must be impressed on all ranks.

[signature]

Major.
Bde.Major.
230th Inf.Bde.

9th Oct.,1918.

Copies to:-

10th Buffs.
15th Suffolks.
16th Sussex.
230th L.T.M.B.
74th Division.
231st InfBde.
166th Inf.Bde.
87th Bde.R.F.A.
74th M.G.Bn.
File.

SECRET.

Copy No.....6.

Addenda No.2. Brigade Order No.74.

1. L.T.M.B.
The 231st Infantry Brigade have two guns in position at U.5.b.1.8.
This position will be taken over by O.C., 230th L.T.M.B. and the disposition of the other two guns will be disposed after discussion with O.C., Outpost Battalion.

2. Arrangements will be made as far as possible to exchange guns and ammunition.

3. Further details of relief will be made between Os.C.concerned

4. ACKNOWLEDGE.

[signature]

Major,
Brigade Major.
230th Infantry Brigade

9th October 1918.

Copies to:-
No.1. 10th Buffs.
2. 15th Suffolks.
3. 16th Sussex.
4. 230th L.T.M.B.
5. 74th Division.
6. 231st Inf.Bde.
7. 166th Inf.Bde.
8. 87th Bde.R.F.A.
9. 74th M.G.Battn.
10. File.

SECRET. Copy. No.....8...

230th Infantry Brigade Order No. 76.

Ref. Map. 1-20000 36 S.W.

1. On the night of 13/14th Oct. the following reliefs will take place:-
   (a). 15th Suffolks will relieve 16th Sussex in the Outpost Line
   (b). 10th Buffs will relieve 15th Suffolks in the Outpost Line of Resistance.
   (c). 16th Sussex will come in reserve and will occupy billets vacated by 10th Buffs.

2. All ~~XXXXXXX~~ photographs, ~~special~~ trench stores, special maps etc., dealing with the Front Line will be handed over.

3. Details of relief will be made between C.Os. concerned.

4. Completion of relief will be wired by code words as follows:-

10th Buffs	Ten available
15th Suffolks	Alright
16th Sussex	Not Possible.

5. ACKNOWLEDGE.

Major.
Bde.Major.
230th Inf.Bde.

12th Oct.,1918.

Copies to:-
1. 10th Buffs.
2. 15th Suffolks.
3. 16th Sussex.
4. 230th L.T.M.B.
5. 229th Inf.Bde.
6. 164th Inf.Bde.
7. 74th Division.
8. File.

SECRET.

Copy No...7...

230th Infantry Brigade Order No. 78.

Reconnaissance of a Main Line of Resistance.

Should the necessity arise the 230th Brigade will hold the following line:-

Road Junction N.23.c.1.4. (Road exc.). to Northern Boundary of Brigade N.17.c.3.9.

This Sector will be sub-divided as follows:-

10th Buffs N.23.c.1.4. (Road exc.) to High Ground Pt.40. (N.23.a.) inclusive.

16th Sussex Pt. 40. (exc.) to N.Boundary N.17.c.3.9.

15th Suffolks in Reserve at BAISIEUX.

O.C. 179 A.F.A.Bde and O.C./"D" Coy M.G.C. will reconnoitre the whole line with a view to covering it.
Battalion Commanders will reconnoitre their respective Sectors.

All reconnaissances will be carried out and detailed reports forwarded to B.H.Q. as early as possible to-morrow morning.

N.B. Brigade Group stands fast, to-night.

ACKNOWLEDGE.

Capt.
Bde.Major.
230th Inf.Bde.

20th Oct.,1918.

Copies to:-

1. 10th Buffs.
2. 15th Suffolks.
3. 16th Sussex.
4. L.T.M.B.
5. 179 A.F.A.Bde.
6. "D" Coy. M.G.C.
7. File.

SECRET.   Copy No.....14

230th Infantry Brigade Order No. 79.

1. 230th Infantry Brigade will relieve 229th Infantry Brigade in the line on the night of 24/25th Oct.,as follows:-

   10th Buffs will relieve 14th R.Highlanders in Front Line.
   16th Sussex the 12th S.L.I. in Support.
   15th Suffolks the 16th Devons in Reserve.
   230th L.T.M.B. the 229th L.T.M.B.

2. "A" Coy., M.G.Bn. will replace "D" Coy., at present attached to 230th Infantry Brigade.

3. On relief Units will be disposed as follows:-

   Bde. H.Q., H.Q. 230th L.T.M.B., H.Q. R.A.,R.E. Section remain in present billets.
   10th Buffs Bn. H.Q., ORCQ, O.26.b.1.5.
   16th Sussex) MAEQUAIN.) Bn. H.Q. to be notified later.
   15th Suffolks)
   "A" Coy. M.G.Bn. H.Q. ~~to be notified later~~. BAISIEUX N19c2.9

4. The Troop King Edward's Horse is being transferred to 230th Infantry Brigade and will join B.H.Q. at BAISIEUX.

5. Artillery reliefs are being arranged separately by C.R.A.

6. The Tunnellers at present attached to the 229th Infantry Brigade will on relief be transferred to the 230th Infantry Brigade.

7. All details of relief will be arranged direct between Commanding Officers concerned.

8. Completion of relief will be wired to this Office using the code word "FOX".

9. ACKNOWLEDGE. (Addressees only).

D C Gilroy
Capt.
Bde.Major.
230th Inf.Bde.

24th Oct.,1918.

Addressed to:-
1. 10th Buffs.
2. 15th Suffolks.
3. 16th Sussex.
4. 230th L.T.M.B.
5. "A" Coy. M.G.C.
6. Section, R.A.,R.E.
7. King Edward's Horse.

Copies to:-
8. 74th Division.
9. 229th Inf.Bde.
10. 231st Inf.Bde.
11. 164th Inf.Bde.
12. 171st Inf.Bde.
13. War Diary.
14. File.
15. Staff Capt.
16. Bde. Signal. Officer.

7

<u>230TH INFANTRY BRIGADE ORDER NO. ~~...~~ 80</u>

Ref, Sheet 37 - 1/40,000
Ref. D.O.108 - para 3

Should the enemy retire 10th Buffs will push patrols across River ESCAUT by the bridges O.23.a0.6. and 4.7 to O.17.b.5.4. - O.18.a.5.0. P.13.c.8.2. and along railway to P.19.b.8.2.

Lewis Guns and later M.Gs will be sited on bridges O.23.a.0.6. and 4.7. to cover a possible withdrawal.

Patrols must be backed up by successive reinforcements who will hold tactical points until objectives are gained.

The 16th Sussex will follow up, pass through the 10th Buffs, and capture RUMILLIES (P.15.).

After the capture of RUMILLIES 10th Buffs will be responsible for the defence of the line P.13.c.8.2. to O.17 central.

16th Sussex will be responsible for the line from railway P.16.c.0.0 - P.15.a.8.8., thence N. of road to P.13.c.8.2.

As soon as 16th Sussex have established their line 10th Buffs will withdraw any troops holding the line P.19.b.8.2. - P.13.c.8.2.

16th Suffolks will be held in reserve.

16th Sussex and 15th Suffolks will move under orders from B.H.Q.

Bde
O.C. 117 R.F.A. will be prepared to cover this advance.

Sect. R.A.R.E. will arrange to move forward under B.H.Q. orders for bridging purposes.

O.C. A Coy M.G. Bn will arrange for one section tomove forward with 10th Buffs.

One section will accompany the 16th Sussex when ordered to move.

The two remaining sections will be under the orders of B.H.Q.

<u>Acknowledge.</u>

October 25th 1918.

D C Gilbey
Capt.
Brigade Major,
230th Infantry Brigade

Copies to:-

~~Suffolks~~

Buffs	Suffs
Sussex	A Coy M.G. Bn
Sect. R.A.R.E.	117 R.F.A. Bde.
74th Div.	231st Bde.
File.	230th L.T.M.B.

<u>SECRET.</u> Copy No. 19

230th Infantry Brigade Operation Order No. 91.

Ref. Sheet 37 1/40,000.

1. On the night of 28/29th Oct., the 15th Suffolks and the 16th Sussex will relieve the 10th Buffs in the Front Line.

2. The 15th Suffolks will be on the Right and the 16th Sussex. on the left.
Each Batt., in addition to holding the Front Line, will hold the Outpost Line of Resistance, putting two Coys. in each Line.
The 10th Buffs will come into Brigade Reserve and billet in Marquain.

3. The Boundary Line between these two Battns. will be approximately and East and West Line through O.19.d.0.5.

4. Details of Relief and Sectors to be held will be arranged between Commanding Officers concerned.

5. All maps, etc. will be handed over.

6. Battn. Headquarters, of 15th Suffolks, 16th Sussex and 10th Buffs will all be in MARQUAIN.

7. Relief complete will be reorted to B.H.Q. by code word "TO GROUND".

8. ACKNOWLEDGE.

Capt.
Bde.Major.
230th Inf.Bde.

27th Oct.,1918.

Copies to:-

1. B.G.C.
2. 10th Buffs.
3. 15th Suffolks.
4. 16th Sussex.
5. 230th L.T.M.B.
6. "A" Coy. M.G.Bn.
7. Section R.A., R.E.
8. 44th R.F.A.Bde.
9. 165th Inf.Bde.
10, 172 Inf.Bde.
11. 74th Division.
12. 231st Fld.Amb.
13. 439 Fld. Coy.R.E.
14. 251 Tunnelling Coy. R.E.
15. Bde.Major.
16. Staff Capt.
17. Bde.Signal Officer.
18-19. War Diary.
20. File.

SECRET.   Copy. No..20..

Amendment No. 1 to 230th Infantry Brigade Operation Order No-82.

Para. 10 is cancelled and the following is substituted:-

On "A" Battn. moving forward, the 2 Companies of "B" Battn. holding the forward line will retain their defensive position in front of ORCQ. The 2 Companies of "B" Battn. holding the Outpost Line of Resistance will at once move forward to ORCQ in Support of the 2 Companies already named.

The following addition is made.

All transport will move under orders of Battn. Commanders.

D C Galway

Capt.
Bde. Major.
230th Inf. Bde.

29th Oct., 1918.

Copies to all Recipients of Order No. 82.

SECRET. Copy No. 20

230th Infantry Brigade Operation Order No. 82.

Reference Map:- Sheet 37, 1/40,000.

1. Owing to reliefs B.O. No.80 is cancelled.

2. For the purpose of a forward move Battalions will be lettered as follows:-

16th Sussex.	"A"
15th Suffolks.	"B"
10th Buffs.	"C"

3. Should the enemy retire "A" Battalion will push patrols across the River ESCAUT by the bridges 0.23.a.0.6. and 4.7. to 0.17.b.5.4. 0.18.a.5.0., P.13.c.8.2. and along railway to P.19.b.8.2.

4. Lewis Guns and later M.G's will be sited on bridges 0.23.a.0.6.and 4.7. to cover a possible withdrawal.

5. Patrols must be backed up by successive reinforcements who will hold tactical points until objectives are gained.

6. "B" Battn. will follow up, pass through "A" Battn.,and capture RUMILLIES (P.15).

7. After the capture of RUMILLIES "A" Battn., will be responsible for the defence of the Line P.13.b.8.2.exclusive to 0.17.central.

8. As soon as "B" Battn., have established their Line, "A" Battn., will withdraw any troops holding the Line P.19.b.8.2. - P.13.c.8.2.
One Coy., of "C" Bn., will at once move forward crossing the River by the bridges in 0.23.a.0.6. and 4.7. and picket all the exits of TOURNAI East of the River from 0.23.a.0.6., where a mixed picket will be formed with the 231st Inf.Bde., to 0.30.c.8.3. and here it will establish a mixed post with the 55th Division. The duty of these pickets will be to prevent all civilians from leaving Tournai on any pretext.

9. "C" Bn.,less one Coy., will form Brigade Reserve.

10. On "A" Battn., moving forward, "B" Battn., will move to ORCQ and there take up a defensive position.

11. As soon as "B" Battn., vacates ORCQ it will be replaced by "C" Battn.

12. "B" and "C" Battns., will move under orders from B.H.Q.

13. B.H.Q. will open an advance Report Centre at ORCQ, 0.26.b.2.3. as soon as a forward movement commences.

14. O.C. "A" Coy., M.G.Bn., will detail one Section to accompany each Battalion,the remaining Section forming Brigade Reserve and moving under orders from B.H.Q.

15. O.C. 44th R.F.A.,Bde., will cover this advance and arrange S.O.S. barrage on objectives being gained.

16. O.C. Section R.A.,R.E. will send forward a small party with "A" Battn.
Bridging party to move forward under orders from B.H.Q.

17. O.C. 251 Tunnelling Coy.R.E. will detail parties to accompany "A" and "B" Battns., and will arrange for the examination of all bridges in area controlled by 230th Infantry Brigade.

18. 230th L.T.M.B. will accompany transport of B.H.Q.

19. ACKNOWLEDGE.

D C Gilroy
Capt,
Brigade Major.
230th Infantry Brigade.

27th October 1918.

Copies to:-
No.1. B.G.C.
2. 10th Buffs.
3. 15th Suffolks.
4. 16th Sussex.
5. 230th L.T.M.B.
6. "A" Coy.,M.G.Battn.
7. Section R.A.,R.E.
8. 251 Tunnelling Coy.,R.E.
9. 44th R.F.A.Bde.
10. 165 Inf.Bde.
11. 172 Inf.Bde.
12. 74th Division.
13. 231st Inf.Bde.
14. 229th Inf.Bde.
15. 439 Fld.Coy. R.E.
16. Bde.Major.
17. Staff Capt.
18. Bde.Signal Officer.
19-20. War Diary.
21. File.

<u>NOTE</u>. Reference para 2, should the enemy withdraw before the Battalion relief takes place night of 28th/29th Battalions will be lettered as follows :-

10th Buffs.	"A"
16th Sussex.	"B"
15th Suffolks.	"C"

SECRET. Copy No. 20

230th Inf.Brigade Order No. 83.

Reference Sheet 37 1/40,000.

1. On the night of 30/31 Oct., 230th Infantry Brigade is being relieved in the Forward Zone by 231st Infantry Brigade.

   On relief 230th Infantry Brigade will come into Divisional Reserve be responsible for holding the Main Line of Resistance and will take over the duty in connection with the occupation of TOURNAI, for which instructions will be issued later.

2. 15th Suffolks are being relieved by 10th K.S.L.I., 16th Sussex by 24th Welsh, 10th Buffs by 25th R.W.F. and will occupy the Billets vacated by those Units respectively.

   10th K.S.L.I. are billeted at HAUDION, 24th Welsh at LAMAIN, 25th R.W.F. at HERTAIN.

   Battalions will send parties to take over billets from opposite numbers on Oct.,30th.

   231st Inf.Brigade are adopting a similar policy with Reserve Battn., of 230th Inf.Brigade and are also sending advance Parties to each Battalion in the line at 1600 Oct.,29th, disposed as follows:-

   1 Officer 2 N.C.Os. per Battn. H.Q.
   1 Officer per Company.
   1 N.C.O. per Platoon.

3. All details will be arranged between Commanding Officers concerned.

4. 230th and 231st L.T.M.Bs. will arrange dispositions and a mutual exchange of guns.

5. "A" Coy., M.G.Bn. will be relieved under orders from O.C. 74th M.G.Bn.

6. All maps, aeroplane photos, etc, will be handed over.

7. No troops will leave billets before 1700 Oct.,30th.

8. The Command of the Forward Zone will be taken over by B.G.C. 231st Inf.Bde. on completion of relief.

9. 230th Inf.Bde. H.Q., H.Q. 230th L.T.M.B. and Section R.A.,R.E. will remainin present billets at BAISIEUX.

12, Relief complete will be reported ~~by~~ to B.H.Q. by code word "[illegible]".

11. ACKNOWLEDGE.

D C Gilroy
Capt.
Bde.Major.
230th Inf.Bde.

29th Oct.,1918.

Copies to:-

1. B.G.C.
2. 10th Buffs.
3. 15th Suffolks.
4. 16th Sussex.
5. 230th L.T.M.B.
6. "A" Coy M.G.Bn.
7. Sect. R.A.,R.E.
8. 44th R.F.A.Bde.
9. 165th Inf.Bde.
10. 172nd Inf.Bde.
11. 74th Division.
12. 229th Inf.Bde.
13. 231st Inf.Bde.
14. 439 Fld.Coy. R.E.
15. 251 Tunnelling Coy.R.E.
16. Bde.Major.
17. Staff Capt.
18. Bde.Signal Officer.
19-20. War Diary.
21. File.

SECRET.

Copy.NO.....615

Amendment No. 1 to
230th Infantry Brigade Special Instructions

for the
Administration of TOURNAI.

---

1. Para. 18 should read, The French and Belgian and Missions etc. etc.

2. Para. 20 is cancelled.

Capt.
Bde.Major.
230th Inf.Bde.

3rd Nov.,1918.

Copies to all Recipients of above Instructions.

SECRET. Copy No. 16.....

Amendment No. 1 to
230th Infantry Brigade Special Instructions
for the
Administration of TOURNAI.

---

1. Para. 18 should, read The French and Belgian Missions etc. etc.

2. Para. 20 is cancelled.

D C Gibney
Capt.
Bde. Major.
230th Inf. Bde.

3rd Nov., 1918.

Copies to all Recipients of above Instructions.

SECRET. Copy No. 16......

Ref. 37
S.W.
1/20,000
and Special
Map.

230th Infantry Brigade Special Instructions

for the

Administration of TOURNAI.

The 230th Infantry Brigade will be called the Tournai Brigade.

1. RESPONSIBILITY.

The B.G.C. has been appointed the Military Governor of TOURNAI and its suburbs, with responsibility for ~~the~~ maintaining order, closing the entrances into the Town, finding the necessary guards and issuing passes.

For this purpose the Brigade will be utilised.

2. SECTORS.

The enceinte of the Town will be divided into 3 Sectors, for which Battalions of the Brigade will be responsible as under:-

"A" Sector. 16th Suffolks billeted about the STATION or Fg. de MORELLE.
From Bridge at O.23.a.0.6. exclusive to road junction at O.30.b.05.92. exclusive.

"B" Sector. 16th Sussex billeted in the INFANTRY BARRACKS in O.35.b.
From road junction O.30.b.05.92. inclusive to Cross roads at O.29.d.25.30. inclusive.

"C" Sector. 10th Buffs billeted in Fg. de LILLE.
From Cross Roads O.29.d.25.30. exclusive to Bridge at O.23.a.0.6. inclusive.

Posts in "A" Sector will be lettered N (North) those in B Sector S (South) those in "C" Sector W (West).

All Posts will be numbered from Right to Left, in each Sector.

3. PICQUETS AND POSTS.

Picquets and Posts will be established in each Sector as shown in the attached Special Map.

Each Picquet will be under the Command of an Officer.

Officers Commanding Sectors will be responsible that Posts, additional to those on the Special Map, are established on other entrances if necessary.

Posts considered unnecessary will not be withdrawn without reference to Brigade Headquarters.

4. OCCUPATION OF SECTORS.

As soon as the advance commences the TOURNAI Brigade will be ready to advance into TOURNAI.

Orders for this advance will be issued from B.H.Q. and will be carried out as follows, each Unit finding its customary local protection whilst moving into position.

(a). As soon as 231st Infantry Brigade have crossed L'ESCAUT RIVER, 10th Buffs will receive orders to occupy "C" Sector and will form a mixed post with 231st Infantry Brigade on the bridge at O.23.a.0.6.

(b). 16th Sussex will receive orders to occupy that portion of "B" Sector West of the River, and will cross the River by the bridge at O.30.c.85.30. as soon as possible and relieve picquets of 231st Infantry Brigade in the remainder of the Sector.

(c). As soon as 231st Infantry Brigade have established a bridgehead about Fg. du CHATEAU 15th Suffolks will receive orders to cross L'ESCAUT River N. of the Town and take over "A" Sector from troops of 231st Infantry Brigade.

Simultaneously with the above movements Battalions will send forward parties to arrangefor billets in the areas named in para. 2.

5. TUNNELLERS.

251 Tunnelling Coy. R.E. will send forward a party with each Battalion and detail a small party to accompany B.H.Q.

6. POSTS.

Posts on roads will not allow any civilians to leave the Town and will prevent all entry into the Town with the exception of:-

(1). Persons furnished with passes by H.Q. 230th Infantry Brigade, signed by a Staff Officer and bearing the Office Stamp.

(2). All cars carrying authorised flags:-

i.e. Commander-in-Chief	Union Jack.
General Headquarters Staff	Blue and Red.
Army Commander	Black and Red.
Corps Commander	Red with White Cross
Divisional Commander	Red.

Formed bodies of troops marching through and not stopping in the Town will be covered by one pass in the possession of the Officer Commanding.
This does not affect the Special Parties detailed in para. 15.

7. BRITISH TROOPS.

Any British Officer or man found coming out of the Town without a pass will be arrested and sent under escort to Brigade Headquarters.

8. EXAMINING POSTS.

The Officer in Command of each Picquet will establish an Examining Post at his Picquet H.Q. where Parties without passes will be conducted.

9. LEWIS GUNS.

2 Lewis Guns will accompany each Picquet and be sited so as to bear on the entrances to the Town.

10. INLYING PICQUET.

Each Battalion will detail an Inlying Picquet of one Company daily, which will be ready to turn out at half an hour's notice, and will also be available as Fire Picquet.
Orders for the action of the Inlying Picquet will, except in case of extreme emergency, be issued by Brigade H.Q.

11. GUARDS.

(a). Pending the allotment to the Battalions of Guard Duties within the Town
O.C. 10th Buffs will place guards (1Cpl. and 3 Ptes) as soon as possible on
(1) The Post and Telegraph Office.
(2) The Town Hall.

GUARDS. (Cont'd.

(b). O.C. 16th Sussex will place similar guards on the bridge (if existing) at O.30.a. 0.4. and on the Palace of Justice.

(c). O.C. 15th Suffolks will place similar guards on the railway Station; and on the Bridges in O.23.c. and d. and O.29.b. if existing.

12. GRAND ROUNDS.

All Posts will be visited be Grand Rounds (Field Officer or Captain of the day) who will report daily to B.H.Q. This Officer will be detailed consecutively by the 10th Buffs, 16th Sussex and 15th Suffolks in the order named and will commence his duties on the occupation of TOURNAI by the TOURNAI Brigade.

The Battalion Orderly Officer will visit Battn. Posts night and day.

13. BOOBY TRAPS.

Guards and Sentries will be kept well clear of the entrances of buildings, bridges etc which they are guarding until these have been examined by the Tunnellers and reported clear of mines and booby traps.

14. TOWN MAJOR.

Lieut. Colonel G. SHANNON, Nova Scotia Regt. has been appointed Town Major to deal with all civil matters including billeting.

15. SPECIAL PARTIES.

Arrangements will be made as early as possible by the Town Major for billeting the following in the Town:-

(a).	Town Major and Staff. Administartive and Clerical Staff) Cooks, Servant, orderlies and guides) to be provided by battalions of this Brigade) Details follow.) Fire Picquet (Sergt. and 10 Ptes) to be detailed by 15th Suffolks.	50 (approx)
(b).	French and Belgian Mission Personnel.	30 (approx)
(c).	One and a hlaf Sects. 251st Tunnelling Coy. R.E.	100 (approx)
(d).	Medical Detachment. (1 Dressing Station and Aid Post)	20 (approx)
(e).	A.P.M's Detachment.	20 (approx)

The O.C. of each of the above Detachments will submit to Brigade Headquarters the Nominal Roll of Officers and Other Ranks in his Detachment who will require passes to pass in and out of the Town. Those who are not to have passes, but will remain on duty in the Town, will be marched in under an Officer. (vide para. 5).

16. RATIONS.

The Detachments enumerated above, less the Detachment 251st Tunnelling Coy., will be rationed by 10th Buffs.

The Detachments will take with them rations for the day after arrival and will report exact ration strengths to the Town Major immediately on arrival.

17. EXAMINATION OF SUSPECTS, etc.
The arrest and examination of Suspects will be carried out under the orders of A.P.M. III Copps, whose location will be notified later.

18. FRENCH MISSION.
The French Mission, accompanied by certain Staff Officers specified on the pass, willbe allowed to enter the Town by the Gate at O.28.b.6.7. as soon as it has been captured.

19. ESTAMINETS.
Immediately after TOURNAI has been occupied, all Estaminets, Cafes, and other places where wine, spirits and other alcoholic liquor is sold will be closed pending the issue of further orders.

20. ATTACHED TROOPS.
As soon as the above orders come into force the remaining troops of the 230th Brigade Group (less Tunnellers) will revert to Divisional control.

21. HEADQUARTERS.
Headquarters of 230th Infantry Brigade and of the Military Governor will be in the Fg. de LILLE.

22. ACKNOWLEDGE.

D.C. Gilroy Capt.
Bde.Major.
230th Inf.Bde.

30th Oct.,1918.

Copies to:-

1. B.G.C.
2. 10th Buffs.
3. 15th Suffolks.
4. 16th Sussex.
5. 230th L.T.M.B.
6. 251 Tunnelling CoY.
7. 44th R.F.A. Bde.
8. 74th Division.
9. 229th Inf.Bde.
10. 231st Inf.Bde.
11. Lt.Col. Shannon.
12. Bde.Major.
13. Staff Capt.
14. Bde.Signal Off.
15-16. War Diary.
17. Spare.
18. "
19. "
20. "
21. "

SECRET. Copy No. 19

Amendment No. 1 to 230th Infantry Brigade Order No. 84.

Para. 2 will be altered as follows:-

(b). 16th Sussex will hold etc., etc.

Para 3 will be altered as follows:-

(b). Troops of the 230th Infantry Brigade etc., etc.

15th Suffolks will remain in Reserve at HALT HOUSE (H.10.c) etc., etc.

ACKNOWLEDGE.

Capt.
Bde.Major.
230th Inf.Bde.

6th Nov.,1918.

Copies to all Recipients of Order No. 84.

SECRET. Copy No.19...

230th Infantry Brigade Order No. 84.

Ref. Sheet 37. 1/20.000

1. 231st Infantry Brigade Order No. 81 handed over to Battalions on Relief will hold good, with the following alterations.

2. Para 2 will read as follows:-

230th Infantry Brigade is responsible for the defence of the Main Line of Resistance.

(a).10th Buffs will hold the line from the BAISIEUX - MARQUAIN road exclusive to the Northern Divisional Boundary.

(b).15th Suffolks will hold from the BAISIEUX - MARQUAIN road inclusive to the Southern Divisional Boundary.

(c).O.C. 230th L.T.M.B. will select emplacements to cover the above line

(d).O.C. "B" 74th M.G.Bn. will dispose his guns in depth to cover this line as far W as the BLANDAIN (N.16.c) - QUATRE CHEMINS (T.3.b) road exclusive.

(e).O.C. "A" Coy. 74th M.G.Bn. will dispose his guns in depth between the BLANDAIN - QUATRE CHEMINS road inclusive and the line BAISIEUX - CAMPHIN.

Para 3 will read as follows:-

(b).Troops of the 230th Infantry Brigade Group as detailed in para 2 will man Battle Stations.
16th Sussex will remain in reserve at LAMAIN, etc etc.

4. 10th Buffs, 15th Suffolks, 230th L.T.M.B.,"A" and "B" Coys 74th M.G.Bn. will forward maps showing exact dispositions to reach B.H.Q. by 1800 1st Nov.

5. ACKNOWLEDGE.

Capt.
Bde.Major.
230th Inf.Bde.

31st Oct.,1918.

Copies to:-

1. B.G.C.
2. 10th Buffs
3. 15th Suffolks.
4. 16th Sussex.
5. 230th L.T.M.B.
6. "A" Coy. M.G.Bn.
7. "B" Coy. M.G.Bn.
8 166th Inf.Bde.
9. 173 Inf.Bde.
10. 74th Division.
11. 74th M.G.Bn.
12. 229th Inf.Bde.
13. 231st Inf.Bde.
14. Bde.Major.
15th Staff Capt.
16th Bde.Signal Offr.
17. I.O.
18-19 War Diary.
20. Spare.
21. Spare.

SECRET. B.M.A. 30.

D E F E N C E   S C H E M E.

1. The Brigade will be distributed in depth.
Two Battns. holding the Front Line and Outpost Line of Resistance- one Battn. in Reserve.

2. Forward Battns. will have two Companies in the Front Line and two Companies in the Outpost Line of Resistance.
The Reserve Battn. will be billeted in MARQUAIN, and ready to move at half an hour's notice.
Headquarters of all three Battns. will be in MARQUAIN.
Bde.H.Q. will remain at Chateau d'ESCANIN, BAISIEUX.
"A" Coy. M.G.Bn. will have one Section in the Front Line, two Sections in the Outpost Line of Resistance and one Section in Reserve in MARQUAIN ready to move into position at half an hour's notice.
L.T.M.B. will be distributed as required in the Front Line.
44th R.F.A. Bde., will be distributed in depth to cover the Front and will also arrange suitable positions for the M.T.M.B.

3. In the event of a hostile attack the Front Line troops will deal with all minor enterprises. Should the attack be general they will retire fighting to the Outpost Line of Resistance.
The Outpost Line of Resistance will be maintainedby utilising all available Brigade Resources.
No withdrawal from this line will take place except under orders from B.H.Q.

4. ACKNOWLEDGE.

D C Gilroy
Capt.
Bde.Major.
230th Inf.Bde.

28th Oct.,1918.

Copies to:-

B.G.C.
10th Buffs.
15th Suffolks.
16th Sussex.
230th L.T.M.B.
"A" Coy. M.G.Bn.
44th R.F.A.Bde.
74th Division.
165th Inf.Bde.
172nd Inf.Bde.
War Diary.
File.

SECRET. Copy No....10....

Amendment No. 1 to
230th Infantry Brigade Special Instructions

for the
Administration of TOURNAI.

---

1. Para. 18 should read, The French and Belgian Missions etc. etc.

2. Para. 20 is cancelled.

D C Gibney
Capt.
Bde.Major.
230th Inf.Bde.

3rd Nov.,1918.

Copies to all Recipients of above Instructions.

SECRET.   Copy No.....10

230th Infantry Brigade Special Instructions

for the

Administration of TOURNAI.

Ref. 37
S.W.
1/20,000
and special
Map.

The 230th Infantry Brigade will be called the TOURNAI Brigade.

1. RESPONSIBILITY.

The B.G.C. has been appointed Military Governor of Tournai and its suburbs, with responsibility for maintaining order, closing the entrances into the Town, finding the necessary guards and issuing passes.

For this purpose the Brigade will be utilised.

2. SECTORS.

The enceinte of the Town will be divided into 3 Sectors, for which Battalions of the Brigade will be responsible as under:-

"A" Sector. 15th Suffolks billeted about the STATION or Fg. de MORELLE.
From Bridge at O.23.a.0.6. exclusive to road junction at O.30.b.05.92. exclusive.

"B" Sector. 16th Sussex billeted in the INFANTRY BARRACKS in O.35.b.
From road junction O.30.b.05.92. inclusive to Cross roadsat O.29.d.25.30. inclusive.

"C" Sector. 10th Buffs billeted in Fg.de LILLE.
From Cross roads O.29.d.25.30. exclusive to Bridge at O.23.a.0.6. inclusive.

Posts in "A" Sector will be lettered N(North) those in "B" Sector S(South), those in "C" Sector W(West).

All Posts will be numbered from Right to Left in each Sector.

3. PICQUETS AND POSTS.

Picquets and Posts will be established in each Sector as shown in the attached Special Map.

Each Picquet will be under the Command of an Officer.

Officers Commanding Sectors will be responsible that Posts, additional to those shown on the Special Map, are established on other entrances if necessary.

Posts considered unnecessary will not be withdrawn without reference to Brigade Headquarters.

4. OCCUPATION OF SECTORS.

As soon as the advance commences the TOURNAI Brigade will be ready to advance into TOURNAI.

Orders for this advance will be issued from B.H.Q. and will be carried out as follows, each Unit finding its customary local protection whilst moving into position.

(a). As soon as 231st Infantry Brigade have crossed L'ESCAUT RIVER, 10th Buffs will receive orders to occupy "C" Sector and will form a mixed post with 231st Infantry Brigade on the bridge at O.23.a.0.6.

(b). 16th Sussex will receive orders to occupy the portion of "B" Sector West of the River, and will cross the River by the bridge ~~at~~ O.30.c.85.30. as soon as possible and relieve picquets of 231st Infantry Brigade in the remainder of Sector.

(c). As soon as 231st Infantry Brigade have established a bridgehead about Fg.du CHATEAU

OCCUPATION OF SECTORS (Cont'd).

15th Suffolks will receive orders to cross L'ESCAUT River N. of the Town and take over "A" Sector from troops of 231st Infantry Brigade.

Simultaneously with the above movements Battalions will send forward parties to arrange for billets in the areas named in para. 2.

5. TUNNELLERS.

251 Tunnelling Coy. R.E. will send forward a party with each Battalion and detail a small party to accompany B.H.Q.

6. POSTS. Posts on roads will not allow any civilians to leave the Town and will prevent all entry into the Town with the exception of:-

(1). Persons furnished with passes by H.Q. 230th Infantry Brigade, signed by a Staff Officer and bearing the Officestamp.

(2). All cars carrying authorised flags:-

i.e. Commander-in-Chief	Union Jack.
General Headquarters Staff	Blue and Red.
Army Commander	Black and Red.
Corps Commander	Red with white Cross.
Divisional Commander.	Red.

Formed bodies of troops marching through and not stopping in the Town will be covered by one pass in the possession of the Officer Commanding. This does not affect the Special Parties detailed in para. 15.

7. BRITISH TROOPS.

Any British Officer or man found coming out of the Town without a pass will be arrested and sent under escort to Brigade Headquarters.

8. EXAMINING POSTS.

The Officer in Command of each Picquet will establish an Examining Post at his Picquet H.Q. where Parties without passes will be conducted.

LEWIS GUNS.
9. ~~XXXXXXXXXXXXXX~~.

2 Lewis Guns will accompany each Picquet and be sited so as to bear on the entrances to the Town.

10. INLYING PICQUETS.

Each Battalion will detail an Inlying Picquet of one Company daily, which will be ready to turn out at half an hour's notice, and will also be available as Fire Picquet.

Orders for the action of the Inlying Picquet will, except in case of extreme emergency, be issued by Brigade H.Q.

11. GUARDS.

(a). Pending the allotment to the Battalions of Guard Duties within the Town O.C. 10th Buffs will place guards (1 Cpl. and 3 Ptes) as soon as possible on

(1) The Post and Telegraph Office.
(2) The Town Hall.

GUARDS (Cont'd).

(b). O.C. 13th Sussex will place similar guards on the bridge (if existing) at O.30.a.0.4. and on the Palace of Justice.

(c). O.C. 15th Suffolks will place similar guards on the Railway Station; and on the Bridges in O.23.c. and d. and O.29.b. if existing.

12. GRAND ROUNDS.

All Posts will be visited by Grand Rounds (Field Officer or Captain of the day) who will report daily to B.H.Q.

This Officer will be detailed consecutively by the 10th Buffs, 16th Sussex and 15th Suffolks in the order named and will commence his duties on the occupation of TOURNAI by the TOURNAI Brigade.

The Battalion Orderly Officer will visit Bn. Posts night and day.

13. BOOBY TRAPS.

Guards and Sentries will be kept will clear of the entrances of buildings, bridges etc which they are guarding until these have been examined by the Tunnellers and reported clear of mines and booby traps.

14. TOWN MAJOR.

Lieut. Colonel G.SHANNON, Nova Scotia Regt. has been appointed Town Major to deal with all civil matters including billeting.

15. SPECIAL PARTIES.

Arrangements willbe made as early as possible by the Town Major for billeting the following in the Town.:-

(a). Town Major and Staff. — 50 (approx).
Administrative and Clerical Staff cooks, servant, orderlies and guides to be provided by Battalions of this Brigade. Details follow.
Fire Picquet (Sergt. and 10 Ptes) to be detailed by 15th Suffolks

(b). French and Belgian Mission Personnel. — 30 (approx)

(c). One and a half Sects. 251st Tunneling Coy. R.E. — 100 (approx)

(d). Medical Detachment. (1 Dressing Station and Aid Post.) — 20 (approx)

(e) A.P.M's Detachment. — 20 (approx)

The O.C. of each of the above Detachments will submit to Brigade Headquarters the Nominal Roll of Officers and Other Ranks in his Detachment who will require passes to pass in and out of the Town. Those who are not to have passes, but will remain on duty in the Town, will be marched in under an Officer. (vide para.5).

16. RATIONS.

The Detachments enumerated above, less the Detachment 251st Tunnelling Coy., will be rationed by 10th Buffs.

The Detachments will take with them rations for the day after arrival and will report exact ration strengths to the Town Major immediately on arrival.

17. EXAMINATION OF SUSPECTS etc.

The arrest and examination of Suspects will be carried out under the orders of A.P.M. III Corps, whose location will be notified later.

18. FRENCH MISSION.

The French and Belgian Missions, accompanied by certain Staff Officers specified on the pass, will be allowed to enter the Town by the Gate at O.28.b.4.7. as soon as it has been captured.

19. ESTAMINETS.

Immediately after TOURNAI has been occupied, all Estaminets, Cafes, and other places where wine spirits and other alcoholic liquor is sold will be closed pending the issue of further orders.

20. ATTACHED TROOPS.

As soon as the above orders come into force the remaining troops of the 230th Brigade Group (less Tunnellers) will revert to Divisional control.

[Cancelled]

21. HEADQUARTERS.

Headquarters of 230th Infantry Brigade and of the Military Governor will be in the Fg. de LILLE.

22. ACKNOWLEDGE.

Capt.
Bde.Major.
230th Inf.Bde.

30th Oct.,1918.

Copies to:-

1. B.G.C.
2. 10th Buffs.
3. 15th Suffolks.
4. 16th Sussex.
5. 230th L.T.M.B.
6. 251 Tunnelling Coy.
7. 44th R.F.A.Bde.
8. 74th Division.
9. 229th Inf.Bde.
10. 231st Inf.Bde.
11. Lt.Col. Shannon.
12. Bde.Major.
13. Staff Capt.
14. Bde Signal Officer.
15-16. War Diary.
17. Spare.
18. "
19. "
20. "
21. "

Vol. 8.

Headquarters,
230th Inf. Bde.
(74th Division)

November 1918.

D. D. & L., London, E.C.
(P6975) Wt.W11200/H2695 500,000 12/16 W21 H16/580

(69)

COVER

FOR

BRANCH MEMORANDA.

Unregistered.

Referred to	Date.	Referred to	Date
~~229th. Infantry Brigade~~			

Headquarters
74th (Yeo) Division

HEADQUAR
4 DEC 1918

Herewith War Diaries for the month of November in respect of these Headquarters and Units of this Brigade

3/12/18

D C Gething Capt
for Brig. Genl.
Cmdg. 230th. Infantry Brigade

1

230^E Inf Bde

BEF

Instructions regarding War Diaries and Intelligence Summaries are contained in F.S. Regs., Part. II. and the Staff Manual sespectively. Title pages will be prepared in manuscript.

WAR DIARY
or
INTELLIGENCE SUMMARY.
(Erase heading not required).

PAGE. 1
Nov 1918

Army Form C. 2118.

WO 230 Suffolk

Place	Date	Hour	Summary of Events and Information	Remarks and references to Appendices.
	1		During morning BGC and Bde Maj inspected work done + siting of trenches on Main Line of Resistance.	Sheet 37 1/40,000
	2	0100	Heavy Shelling of HAUDION till 0300. Suffolks billeted here	
		1500	Conference of Battn Education officers at BHQ under Div Education Officer.	
	3	1000	During morning BGC + Bm visited 15^E Suffolks + 16^E Sussex	
		1400	Issued Ammendment No1 to Special TOURNAI Instructions.	
	4	1000	BGC inspected ~~15^E Suffolks~~ 10^E Buffs and presented M M Ribbons. Lt C JACKSON RE Sigs from Hospital	
			During the afternoon Bde Major visited 15^E Suffolks + 16^E Sussex.	
	5	1200	Lt H L MERRICK RE Sigs departed	
	6	1030	BGC inspected 16^E Sussex and presented M M Ribbons. During morning 15^E Suffolks from HAUDION to MALT HOUSE (T18c) + 1 Coy 10^E Buffs to BAISIEUX from HERTAIN	
		1800	Issued Ammendment No1 to 230 Inf Bde Order No84, due to the change of billets of 15^E Suffolks. 16^E Sussex to hold right sector of Main Line + 15^E Suffolks come into reserve.	
	8	0730	231 Inf Bde telephoned that the Enemy had retired from TOURNAI. Informed units to be ready to march at 1 Hours notice	
		0945	Ordered 10^E Buffs + 15^E Suffolks to move at 1045 and 16^E Sussex at 1115.	
		1115	Arrived ORCQ – Enemy were on E of ESCAUT + holding it strongly. Informed Units and stopped 15^E Suffolks + 16^E Sussex at MARQUAIN. 10^E Buffs were halted at ORCQ.	
		1345	10^E Buffs moved forward to Fbg de LILLE where they billeted + occupied the western outskirts of TOURNAI to prevent ingress and egress. Some casualties from shelling.	
		1430	BHQ established at O28b3.7 but were later changed to O28b0.9 for the night	
		1600	Lieut MURRAY. T. SMITH 21st Lancers joined BHQ from SAISSEVAL near Amiens as a learner	
	9	0230	Big Fire during the night in TOURNAI. Sent Lt GIBSON RMRE to deal with it.	
		0600	Ordered 16^E Sussex to move up + occupy outskirts (S+SE) of TOURNAI	
		0820	Ordered 15^E Suffolks to move at 0930 + occupy outskirts (N+NE) of TOURNAI	
			The whole day was occupied in issuing passes to TOURNAI.	

D C Gilroy Capt
Bm 230^E Inf Bde

A.P. & S.D., Alex./2009/50025A/II : 17/5M. W.M. & Co.

230^E^ Inf Bde — B.E.F

WAR DIARY or INTELLIGENCE SUMMARY.

(Erase heading not required).

PAGE 2 — Nov 1918

Army Form C. 2118.

Instructions regarding War Diaries and Intelligence Summaries are contained in F.S. Regs., Part. II. and the Staff Manual sespectively. Title pages will be prepared in manuscript.

Place	Date	Hour	Summary of Events and Information	Remarks and references to Appendices.
	9	0915	at 0500 2/Lt LILLEY + 40 OR, 10^E^ Buffs crossed the River ESCAUT. No enemy encountered. All clear as far as 1000 yards E of TOURNAI Stn. Civilians report enemy has retired to ATH + there holds a line	Ref Sheet 37, 1/40,000
	10		Passes for TOURNAI issued all day.	
		2235	Issued orders for Brigade to move East at 0900 on 11^E^ + informed them that 141 Inf Bde would relieve them.	
	11	0845	Division telephoned that Hostilities were to cease at 1100 and ordered Bde to stand fast.	
		0945	Bde ordered to move as previously arranged. Warned units + arranged to move at 1130	
		1600	BHQ established at L 25c 8.3 (near DIME) and units as follows. 10^E^ Buffs at BARBERIE (K26) 15^E^ Suffolks L 25 + Eastwards. 16^E^ Sussex PIRE + DIME. 230 LTMB DIME. A Coy MG and 251 Tunnelling Coy RE at HACQUEGNIES.	
	12	0108	Warning order to move early this morning. Informed units.	
		0430	Issued orders to units to move. Leading unit to pass Starting Point HACQUEGNIES Xroads 0930.	
		1600	BHQ established CORNET (B25d 4.5), also {A Coy MG Bn + 230 LTMB} RMRE. 10^E^ Buffs in area G3 + 8 15^E^ Suffolks LAHAMAIDE (B26), 16^E^ Sussex in G5 + A30.	Ref Sh: 38 1/40,000
	13		Brigade repaired main roads in area of billets	
	14	1000	ROKO moved to HERQUEGIES (Sheet 37 R2) to work under 42 AT Coy RE. Remainder of Brigade continued work on road.	
	15	1430	BGC inspected 15^E^ Suffolks at LAHAMAIDE and presented Medal Ribbons	
		1710	Issued march orders for Westward move tomorrow to new Area about THIMOUGIES (Sheet 37)	Sheet 37 1/40000
	16	0945	Brigade moved to new area + was established as follows. BHQ, 230 LTMB + 16^E^ Sussex at THIMOUGIES. 10^E^ Buffs at HERQUEGIES, 15^E^ Suffolks at PIRE + MONTROEUL au BOIS, RMRE at PETRIEUX 251 Tunnelling Coy RE at GRANDE MASURE, 230 Field Ambulance FRASNES, No 3 Coy Div Train BOISSAC.	
	17		Brig Gen AA KENNEDY CMG assumed command of Div vice Major Gen GIRDWOOD on leave	
	18	1130	Battn Comdrs conference at BHQ. 10^E^ Buffs moved to fresh billets in BARRY (W5) area, 15^E^ Suffolks to MANSART (Q35) area in order to work on the Railway. Sect 251 Tunn Coy returned to its unit	

D C Gilroy Capt B.M. 230 Inf Bde

A.P. & S.D., Alex./ 2000/50025A /11 : 17/5M. W.M. & Co.

230 Inf Bde

B.E.F

Instructions regarding War Diaries and Intelligence Summaries are contained in F. S. Regs., Part II. and the Staff Manual respectively. Title pages will be prepared in manuscript.

WAR DIARY or INTELLIGENCE SUMMARY. Nov 1918

(Erase heading not required.)

PAGE 3

Army Form C. 2118.

Place	Date	Hour	Summary of Events and Information	Remarks and references to Appendices
	19		BGC visited 10th Buffs + 15th Suffolks work on LEUZE-TOURNAI Rly + 16th Sussex on Road Craters.	
	20	1100	Education Conference at Div Hd Qrs. After lunch the BGC visited the Corps Commander at TOURNAI	
	21	1000	Lieut H. BROWN Sussex Yeomanry joined as Act Staff Capt vice CAPT MONTGOMERY on leave	
	25th	1200	Lieut C.W. HICKSON, 10th Buffs joined BHQ as Brigade Education Officer	
	20 to 30th		10th Buffs + 15th Suffolks continued work on Railway. 16th Sussex on Roads.	

D C Gilroy Capt
Bde Major 230th Inf Bde

D. D. & L., London, E.C.
(20548) Wt W5300/P713 750,000 3/18 E 2688 Forms C/2118/16.

Vol. 9.

Headquarters,
230th Inf Bde.
(74th Division)

December 1918

BRITISH SALONIKA FORCE.

WAR DIARY.

28th Division.

Vol. No.	Unit	Period From	Period To
42.	C. R.E.	1-4-19	30-4-19
40.	449th (North'bn) Field Coy. R.E.	—	—
44.	Divisional Sig. Coy. R.E.	—	—

A.P. & S.D., Ska. 1118/1070/1 1000 14/1/19 Pap.

61Dw

95

Aug '16

BM 26/1a.

Headquarters.
74th (Yeomanry) Division.

Herewith War Diaries for the month of December 1918 for the following Units of this Brigade:-

H.Q. 230th Infantry Brigade.
10th Buffs.
15th Suffolks.
16th Sussex.
230th L.T.M. Battery.

D C Gilroy Capt
for Brigadier General
Cmdg 230th Infantry Brigade.

6th January 1919.

Dec 18

230th Inf Bde

WAR DIARY
or
INTELLIGENCE SUMMARY. DEC 1918

PAGE 1

Army Form C. 2118.

Instructions regarding War Diaries and Intelligence Summaries are contained in F. S. Regs., Part II. and the Staff Manual respectively. Title pages will be prepared in manuscript.

REF

HQ 230 Inf Bde

V8 9

(Erase heading not required.)

Place	Date	Hour	Summary of Events and Information	Remarks and references to Appendices
	1st to 6th		10th Buffs, 15th Suffolks worked on Railway. 16th Sussex worked on Road Craters	
	5		Staff Captain returned from leave, Lt BROWN returned to D.HQ.	
	7	1230	His Majesty King GEORGE inspected the Division on the LEUZE-TOURNAI Road.	
	8		10th Buffs Railway work. 15th Suffolks recreation. 16th Sussex Drill + Recreation	
	9		10th Buffs recreation. 15th Suffolks Railway work. 16th Sussex Education + Agriculture.	
			B.G.C + Bm ~~[illegible]~~ sent on leave to visit places of interest. Lt Col BALSTON	
			10th Buffs commanding the Bde during the absence of B.G.C	
	10th to 14th		10th Buffs, 15th Suffolks worked on Railway. 16th Sussex Drill, Education + Recreation.	
	11		Lorries sent to Back Areas to buy provisions for Christmas Dinners of Troops.	
	12		Bde Major returned from leave.	
	13		Advance billeting parties sent on by lorry to new area GAMMERAGES, ~~H~~ HERINNES	Ref Sheets TOURNAI BRUSSELS 1/100,000
			BIEVENE. Issued March orders for move.	
	15		Bde moved to billets further east. BHQ, LTMB, 230 Field Ambulance, 10th Buffs, 16th Sussex	
			billeted in FRASNES, 15th Suffolks in BUISSENAL, RMRE in CONTREPRE.	
	16		moved to billets further east. BHQ, LTMB, 230 Field Ambulance GHOY. 10th Buffs,	
			15th Suffolks LES DEUX ACREN. 16th Sussex OGY. RMRE SCAUBECQ.	
	17		Moved to permanent area. BHQ, LTMB, 230 Field Ambulance GAMMERAGES,	
			10th Buffs THOLLEMBEEK, 15th Suffolks HERINNES, 16th Sussex + RMRE BIEVENE.	
			B.G.C returned from leave. Lt Col BALSTON returned to 10th Buffs.	
	18		Lt LEGGE returned to his unit 16th Sussex.	

D C Gilroy Capt
Bm. 230th Inf Bde

D. D. & L., London, E.C.
(10340) Wt W5300/P713 750,000 3/18 E 2688 Forms C/2118/18.

Army Form C. 2118.

Instructions regarding War Diaries and Intelligence Summaries are contained in F. S. Regs., Part II. and the Staff Manual respectively. Title pages will be prepared in manuscript.

230 Inf Bde

B.E.F.

WAR DIARY
or
INTELLIGENCE SUMMARY.
(Erase heading not required.)

Page 2

Dec 1918

Place	Date	Hour	Summary of Events and Information	Remarks and references to Appendices
	19th to 31st		All units of the Brigade employed in Drill, Education + Recreation.	
	20		RMRE changed billets from BIEVENE to St PIERRE CAPELLE	Ref Sheet TOURNAI 1/100,000
	22		Lt JACKSON, Bde Signalling Officer went on leave to U.K.	
	24		BGC + Staff Capt reconnoitred a new Area for Billets at FLOBECQ + ELLEZELLES	
	27		Lt MURRAY SMITH, 21st Lancers, attd to BHQ on leave to U.K.	
	28		Lt ATKINSON, 10th Buffs attd BHQ during the absence of Lt MURRAY SMITH	

D C Gilroy Capt
Bm 230th Inf Bde

D. D. & L., London, E.C.
(20340) Wt W3300/P713 750,000 3/18 E 2688 Forms C/2118/16.

Hd Qrs 230 Inf Bde

230 Inf Bde — BEF

Instructions regarding War Diaries and Intelligence Summaries are contained in F. S. Regs., Part II. and the Staff Manual respectively. Title pages will be prepared in manuscript.

WAR DIARY
or
INTELLIGENCE SUMMARY. Jan 1919

PAGE 1

(*Erase heading not required.*)

Army Form C. 2118.

Jan 1919

VR 10

Place	Date	Hour	Summary of Events and Information	Remarks and references to Appendices
	1 to 31		All units in the Brigade engaged in Education, Drill + Sports	
	1		Captain MONTGOMERY, Staff Captain went on Special Leave to U.K.	
	2nd 3rd		Brigadier on Court of Enquiry at GRAMMONT	
	4th		Recommendations for Honours + Awards, Peace Despatch, forwarded to Divisional HQ	
	8		All horses in Brigade classified by A.D.V.S.	
	9		Brigadier departed to TOURNAI in continuation of GRAMMONT Court of Enquiry.	
	10		Recommendations for ROUMANIAN Decorations sent to Div HdQrs	
	11		Divisional Concert Party visited BHQ.	
	12		Brigadier returned from TOURNAI.	
	14		Brigadier inspected Sussex Transport	
	15		Conference of Brigadiers at 231 BHQ GRAMMONT.	
	16		Staff Capt + Lt MURRAY SMITH returned from leave	
	17		Brigadier went on leave	
	18	1100	Lt Col SPENCE JONES DSO arrived to act as Brigadier	
	20	1500	Conference of COs at BHQ	
	21		Acting Brigadier inspect the Composite Battn of Buffs + Suffolks due to go to BRUSSELS	
	23		B Gen HEATHCOTE inspected the Composite Battn. Further classification of Horses by Remount Board.	
	24		Transport of 10th Buffs proceeded to BRUSSELS by road.	
	25		10th Buffs proceeded to BRUSSELS by buses via NINOVE from VOLLEZEEL.	
	26		Composite Bde of 74th Div marched past King of the Belgians in BRUSSELS. Brig General C.E. HEATHCOTE CMG in command.	

[signature]

D. D. & L., London, E.C.
(10540) Wt W3300/P713 750,000 5/18 E 2588 Forms C/2118/18.

Instructions regarding War Diaries and Intelligence Summaries are contained in F. S. Regs., Part II. and the Staff Manual respectively. Title Pages will be prepared in manuscript.

230 Inf. Bde.
B.E.F.

WAR DIARY
or
~~INTELLIGENCE SUMMARY~~
(Erase heading not required.)

Page 2.

Jan. 1919.

Army Form C. 2118

Place	Date	Hour	Summary of Events and Information	Remarks and references to Appendices
GAMMERAGES	Jan. 28th		10th Buffs rejoined Bde. Group by busses from BRUSSELS. Transport came by road.	
	30.		All animals of the Brigade Group inoculated for "Mallein Test".	

Andrew M. Montgomery
Capt.
Staff Capt.
231 Inf Bde

1875 Wt. W593/826 1,000,000 4/15 J.B.C. & A. A.D.S.S./Forms/C. 2118.

230th L.T.M. Bty.

Army Form C. 2118.

Instructions regarding War Diaries and Intelligence Summaries are contained in F. S. Regs., Part II. and the Staff Manual respectively. Title pages will be prepared in manuscript.

~~WAR DIARY~~
or
INTELLIGENCE SUMMARY.
(Erase heading not required.)

Jan 1919

Place	Date	Hour	Summary of Events and Information	Remarks and references to Appendices
Gammerages	From 1/1/19 to 1/2/19	09.00 - 10.00	Military Parade including Physical Exercise	
		10.00 to 12.00	Education	

H. Pu[illegible] Capt.
O/c 230 L T M B

(A9175) Wt W2358/P360 500,000 12/17 D. D. & L. Sch. 52a. Forms/C2118/15

Instructions regarding War Diaries and Intelligence Summaries are contained in F. S. Regs., Part II. and the Staff Manual respectively. Title pages will be prepared in manuscript.

230 Inf Bde

B.E.F

WAR DIARY
or
INTELLIGENCE SUMMARY.
(Erase heading not required.)

PAGE 1.

FEB 1919

Vol 11

Army Form C. 2118.

Place	Date	Hour	Summary of Events and Information	Remarks and references to Appendices
	2		All "D" Horses despatched to No 3 Veterinary Evacuation Station	
	5.		Brigadier General AA KENNEDY returned from leave & Lt Col Spence JONES left	
	9		Brigadier General AA KENNEDY assumed Command of the Division	
	11		Divisional Cross Country Run at GRAMMONT. Buffs 3rd Place	
	16		Corps Cross Country Run at HAL. Buffs & Sussex Competed	
	24		The Brigadier reassumed Command of the Brigade	
	27		Brigade moved into new billets in GRAMMONT.	
	28		Rapid Demobilisation during month. Brigade about 600 strong.	
			D C Gilroy Capt Brigade Major 230th Inf Bde	

D. D. & L., London, E.C.
(10540) Wt W5300/P713 750,000 5/18 E 2688 Forms C/2118/16.

Army Form C. 2118.

Instructions regarding War Diaries and Intelligence Summaries are contained in F. S. Regs., Part II. and the Staff Manual respectively. Title pages will be prepared in manuscript.

WAR DIARY
or
INTELLIGENCE SUMMARY.
(Erase heading not required.)

230th L.T.M.B.

Place	Date	Hour	Summary of Events and Information	Remarks and references to Appendices
GAMMERACES	1/2/19 to 14/2/19	0900 to 1000	Training Physical Drill	
	"	1000 1200	Education Classes	
	Afternoons Evenings		Sports and Recreations	
	15/2/19		Unit reduced to Cadre Strength	

H. Haughton Lt.

(A9475) Wt W2358/P360 600,000 12/17 D. D. & L. Sch. 52a. Forms/C2118/15

230th Inf Bde

B.E.F

Instructions regarding War Diaries and Intelligence Summaries are contained in F. S. Regs., Part II. and the Staff Manual respectively. Title pages will be prepared in manuscript.

WAR DIARY
or
INTELLIGENCE SUMMARY.
(Erase heading not required.)

PAGE 1

MARCH 1919

Vol 12

14th Qrs 230 Inf Bde

Army Form C. 2118.

MARCH 19

Place	Date	Hour	Summary of Events and Information	Remarks and references to Appendices
	1		Demobilisation of Horses & mules commenced & continued throughout the month	
	3		Despatched Major Buxton's two Horses to Corps Reception Camp (CORCOLO)	
	8		Exchanged two of our good horses for two very bad ones from 8th Division	
	9		Sent 4 Horses & 2 mules for sale to ATH. Three horses returned, 2 too good, 1 not good enough.	
	11		5 mules sent for sale to LESSINES. Three returned unsold.	
	13		Grey mule despatched to CORCOLO for Repatriation to England.	
	16		2 Horses to CORCOLO for sale in France.	
	17		Brig. Gen A A KENNEDY left for ARMY of OCCUPATION to command a Brigade in 3rd NORTHERN DIVISION.	
	22		Wire from QMG stopping all leave, demobilisation etc on account of Strikes in England.	
	23		Buffs & Suffolks moved Billets into another quarter of GRAMMONT.	
	31		Brigade down to Cadre except for 9 retainable men with 15th Suffolks.	
	"		Demobilisation of Officers commenced.	

D C Gilroy Capt
Bde Major 230th Inf Bde

D. D. & L., London, E.C.
(10340) W1 W3300/P713 750,000 3/18 E 2688 Forms C/2118/18.

230th Inf Bde

B.E.F

WAR DIARY
or
INTELLIGENCE SUMMARY.
(Erase heading not required.)

PAGE 1

APRIL 1919

Army Form C. 2118.

Instructions regarding War Diaries and Intelligence Summaries are contained in F. S. Regs., Part II. and the Staff Manual respectively. Title pages will be prepared in manuscript.

Place	Date	Hour	Summary of Events and Information	Remarks and references to Appendices
GRAMMONT	4th		Mobilisation Store Tables ~~also~~ corrected and certain stores inspected by Ordnance Officer, 8th Division.	
	12		Animal account inspected by Colonel Fisher 5th Area and certified correct.	
	14		All X Horses despatched to CORCOL O (Corps Concentration Camp for Horses).	
	25		All X Mules despatched to CORCOL O and not replaced. The Brigade is now without any animals.	
	30		Animal accounts closed	

D C Gilroy Capt.
Bde Major 230 Inf Bde

D. D. & L., London, E.C.
(10340) Wt W3300/P713 750,000 3/18 E 2688 Forms/C2118/12.

230 Inf Bde

Instructions regarding War Diaries and Intelligence Summaries are contained in F. S. Regs., Part II. and the Staff Manual respectively. Title pages will be prepared in manuscript.

B. E. F.

WAR DIARY
or
INTELLIGENCE SUMMARY.
(Erase heading not required.)

PAGE 1

MAY 1919

Army Form C. 2118.

14

Place	Date	Hour	Summary of Events and Information	Remarks and references to Appendices
GRAMMONT	13th		Capt. C W HICKSON, Brigade Education Officer, reported at WIMEREUX as guide to distinguished visitors.	
	16th		Capt D.C GILROY relinquished appointment of Brigade Major on proceeding to U.K.	
			Capt. P.P. KENYON-SLANEY, M.C Royal North Devon Hussars, reported for duty as acting Staff Captain	
	21st		Brigade HQ. Orderly Room was moved to 16 VREDESTRAAT.	
	29th		Orders were received in connection with the further reduction of Cadre 'A' Strengths by 75%.	

P Kenyon-Slaney
Captain
Staff Captain
230th Infantry Bde

D. D. & L., London, E.C.
(10349) Wt W3300/P713 750,000 3/18 E 2688 Forms C/2118/15.

www.ingramcontent.com/pod-product-compliance
Lightning Source LLC
Chambersburg PA
CBHW081357160426
43192CB00013B/2431
* 9 7 8 1 4 7 4 5 3 4 7 0 3 *